Brothers in the
Mekong Delta

D1555014

Brothers in the Mekong Delta

A Memoir of PBR Section 513 in the Vietnam War

GODFREY GARNER

McFarland & Company, Inc., Publishers
Jefferson, North Carolina

LIBRARY OF CONGRESS CATALOGUING-IN-PUBLICATION DATA

Names: Garner, Godfrey, author.
Title: Brothers in the Mekong Delta : a memoir of PBR Section 513 in the
Vietnam War / Godfrey Garner.
Other titles: Memoir of PBR Section 513 in the Vietnam War
Description: Jefferson, North Carolina : McFarland & Company, Inc.,
Publishers, 2020 | Includes index.
Identifiers: LCCN 2020010179 | ISBN 9781476681535 (paperback) ∞
ISBN 9781476639444 (ebook)
Subjects: LCSH: Garner, Godfrey. | United States. Navy. River Patrol Force.
River Section 513. | Vietnam War, 1961–1975—Riverine operations,
American. | Sailors—United States—Biography. | Vietnam War,
1961–1975—Personal narratives, American. | United States.
Navy—History—Vietnam War, 1961–1975. | Vietnam War,
1961–1975—Campaigns—Mekong River Delta (Vietnam and Cambodia)
Classification: LCC DS558.7 .G37 2020 | DDC 959.704/345092 [B]—dc23
LC record available at https://lccn.loc.gov/2020010179

BRITISH LIBRARY CATALOGUING DATA ARE AVAILABLE

ISBN (print) 978-1-4766-8153-5
ISBN (ebook) 978-1-4766-3944-4

© 2020 Godfrey Garner. All rights reserved

*No part of this book may be reproduced or transmitted in any form
or by any means, electronic or mechanical, including photocopying
or recording, or by any information storage and retrieval system,
without permission in writing from the publisher.*

Front cover images: *insets, left to right* David Taylor, Jack Anderson,
Billy Moore and Godfrey Garner; a U.S. Navy river patrol boat
cruises slowly down a canal in the Mekong Delta of South Vietnam
(Arthur Price Collection Tommy Japan 79/Flickr.com).
Background Mekong Delta © 2020 Svetlana Syakina/Shutterstock

Printed in the United States of America

*McFarland & Company, Inc., Publishers
Box 611, Jefferson, North Carolina 28640
www.mcfarlandpub.com*

TABLE OF CONTENTS

Table of Contents

Acknowledgments

All surviving Vietnam veterans owe a debt of gratitude to those who stood beside them—some we knew and some we didn't—who were willing to give their lives for their brothers. We walk and breathe today, we accomplish that which we may, because of these brothers.

Jack Anderson, Billy Moore, David Taylor, and those named in this book kept me alive. More than that, they encouraged me and supported me, as I hope I did for them. We all wrote this memoir, despite the fact that I was the one who put pen to paper. It will hopefully, in some small way, honor those in all our lives. It must be understood, however, that only our brothers at arms can look us in the eye and honestly say, "I know exactly who you are."

It is often said that those who love us suffer the most. Our wives and our children in the years following Vietnam stood by us throughout the healing process, and still do today. Veterans of combat too often unknowingly drive wedges between themselves and those who would love them, eventually alienating those who love them the most. Only the strongest remain.

Of course, our children love us unconditionally because for them it's not necessary to understand. Only the love matters. My children, Temple, Tony, and Glenn, as well as Jack's daughter, Catina, Billy's daughter, Traci, and David's wife, Judy, and daughter, Barbara, are the constants in our lives. Additionally, Jack's daughter, Catina, has blessed and honored me since his death by allowing me to, in some small way, fill the void in her life left by the loss of her father.

Jack's wife, Tina, and Billy's wife, Melody, brought light into their lives as their bodies, in the final days, were wracked with pain from complications the doctors attributed to Agent Orange. Through the years, Melody especially took it upon herself to see that our times together were special and remembered by us all.

Finally, as I grew up without a father, I could never thank enough Jack's father, Vance Anderson, for the calmness and strength with which he took me in as his own. He saw in me a young man struggling to find a sense of direction and self-worth, and, with little more than a hand on my shoulder, stepped into my life and filled a void I didn't even fully understand existed. I'll never be able to repay the fatherly love he gave me and the confidence he instilled in me.

PREFACE:
A FEW SHORT NOTES
FROM YESTERDAY

In the spring of 1967, America's war in Vietnam had been going on for a little more than three years. The first official American troops were sent in 1964 as a response to the Gulf of Tonkin incident. Riverine operations had kicked off in earnest in January of 1967. By the spring of that year, America, in terms of its river and canal operations, hadn't even begun to "understand what they didn't understand" about this type of warfare. Although the first PBR (patrol boat, riverine) had been dropped unceremoniously into the waters of Vietnam the year before, it took months to organize Operation Game Warden, with a mission to deny the enemy access to the rivers and canals of South Vietnam.

This narrative describes riverine operations from the eyes of the men at the pointy end of the spear, aboard these 30-ft long, 10 ft-wide fiberglass ski boats, providing the reader with insights into tactics, techniques, and procedures of PBR operations. More than that, it relates something of the inner lives of the young men who fought on them, many of whom had barely finished high school and had never been in so much as a fistfight back home.

The reader will come away with an understanding of how, in a place and time where miracles dwelled alongside unspeakable tragedies, lifelong bonds and brotherhoods were formed, where the true meaning of "brother" is found.

That spring of 1967, I was truly blessed to find myself among men like Jack Anderson and Billy Moore and David Taylor, as well as all the other members of PBR River Section 513, in Sadec, Vietnam. This memoir explains how we grew to manhood in a short period of time, constantly watching and protecting each other, how we faced horrors and dangers we had never imagined, and how we helped each other emotionally process the after-effects.

1

Preface

Finally, the reader may come to understand the relationships that are formed in combat. How, having miraculously survived the experience of war together, men throughout history have never been never truly whole until they reunite, and can heal each other in ways their loving families never could.

This is not a historical narrative. It's not an explanation of operational strategy. It's a story of a journey—some would say a never-ending journey—that these men undertook together.

PROLOGUE

Seems like Jack always wound up with the fruitcake. It was really a crapshoot and nothing but pure bad luck because everyone just grabbed the next C-rats box in line, but Jack was cursed. At least that's what we all believed. If there was fruitcake in any one of a dozen boxes of C-rations we were given before a patrol, Jack would get it. He just had that cloud hanging over him.

The real problem, however, was that he was cursed in other ways. On average, a patrol would be hit maybe six to eight times a month, depending on where they were assigned and what had been going on in the area. Of course, during Tet and the weeks that followed, that all changed, but normal activity for us dictated around six to eight serious firefights a month.

With Jack, it was different though. Whenever he was on a patrol, everyone just waited for the shit to hit. He just had that "thing." Some folks always hit the jackpot on the slot machines, and some folks always get shot at. It isn't their fault. It's just sort of preordained.

On balance, however, even though Jack had that "cloud thing" going on, he was still the best, and everyone knew it. He was the best at sensing something around the bend in the canal. He was the best shot. He was the one who always stood up and fired when everyone else was reflexively crouching behind the flimsy, fiberglass PBR hulls in the insane hope that the ¼-inch of plastic would stop a bullet, and he possessed the uncanny ability to say "fuck" ten different ways, each conveying a separate, distinct emotion.

Jack had proven that while there were a lot of part-time heroes in the world, the men who made up the roster of PBR Section 513 were among the bravest of the brave. He could always be counted on to pull folks to safety when they'd been wounded. He'd proven it more than once.

Now it must be understood that Vietnam had a way of reaching deep down in you and pulling out something extra, something even you didn't know was there. Insignificant kids routinely woke up one day in Vietnam and became veritable Audie Murphys.

A funny thing happens when you first hear the high-pitched sound of a bullet whizzing by your ear. You experience an instantaneous realization that a human being sent the projectile your way with the full intention that it find its mark. Or you hear a shorter, duller whooshing sound followed immediately by an explosion causing various forms of debris to gush up out of the ground around you. You know that actual sentient human beings are in your midst, and those individuals want nothing more than to end your life.

In a split second, you find yourself subconsciously on the sharpest of fence rails, from which you will definitely fall. The question in that millisecond, the question that courses through your brain at the speed of light is, "Which way will I fall?" The problem is that once you succumb to one way or the other, it is virtually impossible to go back.

You'll hear two voices in that instant. There's always the still, small one that urges you to fall one way, to crawl into the deepest hole you can find and cover your head and ears with your hands. You're familiar with this voice. It's been with you all your life. It's the same voice that cautioned you when you were ten years old against jumping from the swing at its height despite the fact that your friends were daring you. It's the voice that convinced you when you were twelve and had just watched Superman on TV that the bed sheet you had strapped to your back wasn't going to allow you to drift slowly to the ground when you leaped from the roof over your garage. It was a familiar voice and had always kept you relatively safe.

In that instant, however, you'll hear another voice. It's your Vietnam voice. This voice will encapsulate all the messages that have coursed through the minds of heroes the world over throughout history. This voice will literally shove you off the other side of the fence, convincing you that you are brave, courageous, and most of all, that people are depending on you. When you hear that voice, you'll not fall. You'll leap off the fence, and the shield of honor and the grace of God will direct your next few minutes.

Although we were all brave and listened primarily to that second voice, the one that flung us headlong into the breach, Jack was one of those rare young folks who didn't seem to ever hear the first "still, small voice" urging him to find the hole. Most of us accepted that such was not possible for him. That's just who Jack was. But more than that, everyone knew he would be there when we turned to look for a hand to pull us out.

To understand Jack and what set him apart, you had to try and understand all of us. I arrived in Vietnam in the spring of 1967, just a few weeks after Jack and Billy and David and the rest of the guys. They all trained and deployed to Vietnam—fondly referred to by all of us as simply *country*—together. The war in that time had not yet reached that critical point—the one that hit in 1975.

Wars have a fairly predictable evolution, and this one was still in the push/pull phase that some saw as a lull. While we were still engaging the enemy two to three times a week, with some firefights being intense with high losses on both sides, it still seemed like a chess game where your opponent moves and you respond by moving, and on and on. Of course, all that changed the night Tet hit in 1968, but we'll get to that later.

We were all young, and for the most part, arrived in country fairly dumb, for lack of a better term. We were an empty bucket ready to be filled with all that life, such as it was in Vietnam, had to offer. We were kids thrust headlong into the space between the polar opposites of that basic human conflict of doing what is right and doing what is good. We had no idea. We were far from sophisticated enough to comprehend the dichotomy. What we didn't realize early on, however, was that we would throughout our time in country have ample opportunity to contemplate it.

In spite of our very best attempts at optimism, the one thing we all accepted, even if subconsciously, was that we weren't going to make it through an entire year. The odds were just too great. It wasn't a conscious feeling that we carried around us, like a funeral shroud. It was just there, lurking, ready to be pulled out in silent moments of contemplation. The worse feeling, however, was a more conscious, albeit less frequent one. When it hit, you knew it. It was that panicky feeling of being out of control. When that feeling hit you, you looked around for the older, more experienced among you, but all too often, they had the same look. When "loss of control" feelings came around, they weren't subtle; they were harsh and panic-inducing.

Human beings draw confidence and strength from the illusion that they are in control. Combat has a way of stripping that from you. When it begins, when those feelings of loss of control hit you, their arrival is generally signaled by a blast of some type. For us, it was usually a B40 shoulder-fired rocket, followed immediately by the staccato of automatic weapons fire and tracers flying through the air. Of course, occasionally, it seemed a full cacophony of threatening noises and sounds would weave themselves together in a blanket over the entire countryside, then settle gently down upon you until you felt you couldn't breathe, and you entered into a type of confusion you will never experience in any other environment.

The force that thus engulfs you takes away any semblance of authority you may have thought you had over your world. Ironically, it's somehow comforting to know that all you have to do, other than try and fight back, is relax and allow the warmth of this force to carry you to the "great unknown." To paraphrase Bob Dylan, when you have nothing, you've got nothing to lose.

1

FIRST BREATH

The first, fragrant breath of Vietnamese air I inhaled came late one evening in early 1967 as I climbed off the ramp of a C-123 Provider. The plane had inexplicably taxied all the way to the far end of a landing strip at Tan Son Nhut Airfield outside Saigon, swung around heading the opposite direction, and unceremoniously dropped the ramp.

"Okay, you all know where you're going," the crew chief shouted over the roar of the engines, which had not powered down. "Hang around here till first light and grab a ride on a chopper heading your way."

He smiled sardonically, waved, and disappeared into the bowels of the aircraft as the ramp closed, and the plane taxied slowly back toward the opposite end of the runway. Moments later, we tilted our heads back over our shoulders as we watched it climb toward the darkest part of the night sky and away from us.

"Nary a goodbye or go to Hell, huh," Mike Dilmore, a country boy from outside Magee, Mississippi, muttered. "Didn't even stop long enough to refuel."

As the sound of the plane's engines faded, we were confronted by other sounds, which, although we didn't know it at the time, would be with us 24 hours a day for the duration of our stay in Vietnam. Dull explosions and the rapid, staccato tapping of automatic weapons seemed to blanket the night and emanated from various distances and various points throughout the entire countryside.

Tired, a little bewildered, and confused, the five of us who had shared this ride from the Philippine Islands and were each heading for a different location and a different unit just stared out at our new home. Suddenly, the temperature dropped a few noticeable degrees, the air took on a slight chill, and the unmistakable smell of approaching rain forewarned a miserable night to come.

"Rainy season," Mike opined. "We're gonna be drenched in a few minutes."

Brothers in the Mekong Delta

"Over here," shouted Danny Kay, a skinny kid from California who looked like he was ten years old. "Let's get inside one of those," he continued, pointing at a couple of old metal shipping crates about ten feet square.

Euphemistically called "tiger cages," the crates were used to ship virtually all small items into and out of Vietnam. Three of them were lying about in the field at the end of the runway, as if tossed there by an unruly, petulant giant.

We approached slowly, unsure if we might disturb an actual sleeping tiger or cobra. Using the light from Dilmore's Zippo, we dragged our gear in and settled down for a sleepless night, listening to the rain, the sporadic, dull explosions and automatic weapons fire, and wondering to ourselves if we would be one of the two out of ten statistically slated to make it out of Vietnam alive and intact.

We exchanged small talk throughout the night, mostly about home and girlfriends, avoiding discussions or contemplations of what we were to face in the months or years to come. Young men who set foot on the battlefield in Vietnam during that period very quickly come to the realization that their chances of leaving alive and intact were slim. It wasn't a conscious, overbearing thought, but it was there like a small mosquito flicking about your ear, always returning when it had been slapped away. When the subconscious thought became a conscious one, small talk often shifted from "What I'm going to do when I get home," to "What I did before I got here." At some point, all accepted it, and the knowledge calmed them. Unfortunately, many began to drink heavily, smoke the ubiquitous weed, or dabble in heroin, with little concern for long-term consequences.

On this night, however, we were concerned only with staying relatively dry. Dawn brought with it, as it does the world over, feelings of optimism, giving each of us a renewed spirit. It also brought a flock of Huey helicopter gunships which landed close to us as if sent to pick us up. We later learned that that end of the runway was somewhat of a rally point for most of the choppers before taking off across South Vietnam on their daily routines. It also explained why the "Provider" pilot had dropped us there.

The crews of most of the ships jumped to the ground, stretched their limbs, and began fumbling with various pieces of equipment, oblivious to the five guys crawling out of the tiger cage. I slung my M14 over my shoulder, grabbed my gear, and clumsily ambled toward the nearest gunship.

"Hey, man," I shouted over the still whining engine, trying my best to hide my drawl, as well as my apprehension and trepidation. "I need to get to Sadec. Anybody here heading up that way?"

He gave me an expressionless gaze, pointed toward the ground and replied, "It's down, not up." He then slung his finger over his shoulder at another gunship and said, "Check with those guys."

I barely had time to wave goodbye and offer a "good luck" wish to my friends before I found myself sitting on the deck of the chopper with my legs dangling out of the open door. I was holding "white-knuckle-tight" to a pole as the aircraft slipped over the trees then dove back down into a valley and then back up again to clear the treetops on the next hill and back down again. Known as "nap of the earth" (NOE) flight, it was routine to avoid enemy fire.

Thirty minutes later, we landed on a helo pad along a canal off the Mekong River. As we were being waved slowly down by some guy wearing a brown t-shirt and cut off camo pants, I spotted the familiar green PBRs, all tied neatly next to each other at a working pier, like so many little piglets lined up to nurse from a mother sow.

I had trained on the PBRs in northern California for the past few months and was now ready to take my place as a gunner with a crew attached to River Section 513 in Sadec, Vietnam. The PBR was 30 feet long and powered by two diesel engines that ran two Jacuzzi pumps propelling the boat at speeds of more than 35 MPH across the surface of the river, drawing no more than two feet of draft and less at top speed. The Jacuzzi pumps sucked up the river—and the occasional snake swimming too close to the surface—and forced it out the back under immense pressure. Made of fiberglass, the boats were light enough to actually jump earthen barriers between bodies of water and rice paddies, especially during the rainy season. The protection offered by the boat in a firefight was diametrically opposed to the benefit of its light weight, however. Our enemy used very few weapons that were not capable of penetrating a quarter-inch of fiberglass.

The engines, controlled by a set of throttles located by the helm, could be used to steer the boat in case the steering mechanism was destroyed. The boat could pivot on a dime, reverse direction, turn on its own length, or come to a stop from full speed in the distance of a few feet.

My gear and I were unceremoniously deposited on the helo pad. Before I could establish my footing on stable ground, the chopper had lifted off and was airborne, heading south. The gunner had been considerate enough to give me a couple of last-minute instructions.

"You're in Vinh Long," he shouted over the engine roar. "Sadec is up-river a few klicks. The guys here will pass you off to your folks with 513."

Within an hour I was heading north on the Mekong River. I tried to stay out of the way of the crew, who were a little perturbed that they had to stumble around my gear while they carried out their duties. I suddenly realized that I had never loaded my M14.

"Should I load this?" I shouted at the closest crew member.

He acknowledged me with a look of boredom, laced with something approximating mild amusement, and simply turned back to his chore. I looked around a bit sheepishly and fastened a clip into the M14 I had been issued before I left Clark AFB in the Philippines.

"You need to ditch that thing as soon as you get a chance," came a more engaged voice from one of the other crew members. "It's too heavy to use on the boats. Use the M16s when you get into the shit. There'll be no shortage of them on your boat, and they're fine for everything you'll need."

"Hang that thing on a rack under the bow and leave it," he continued, one hand cupped over his mouth as if anyone more than three inches away could have heard what he said.

"If you ever get a chance, toss it over the side," he laughed out loud. "That way, if you get out of here, all you'll have to take back to the States with you is a note from your command saying it was lost in combat."

"Beats the hell out of luggin' that damn thing all the way back to the States," he concluded, gazing at the rifle with barely disguised disdain.

I had trained for months on the PBR in backwater canals around the countryside near San Francisco before leaving the States. Pulling alongside makeshift enemy sampans, being surprised by automatic weapons fire from popguns, and pelted with small bags of flour representing hand grenades was about as close as I had gotten to the real world of combat.

However, as the boat captain, hugging the riverbank, powered the boat to full speed, and the bow lifted gracefully out of the water, I knew I was in a new game. Throughout the short 30-klick ride upriver to Sadec, I scanned the riverbank for the attack that I was sure would come, and I was equally sure would leave me wounded or dead.

Although I didn't realize it at the time, that feeling was common, and while it would lessen to some extent, it would never cease altogether. It was the beginning of a foregone conclusion, common to all in Vietnam, that you would never leave in the same state you arrived, and based on statistics might never leave at all.

1. First Breath

All too soon, the engine powered back, the bow dropped, and the canal entrance to Sadec came into view. Set at an almost perfect right angle to the mighty Mekong River, I didn't even see the relatively narrow entrance that led west into the village of Sadec until we had turned and powered down to a crawl as we entered. The canal, no more than two hundred yards wide, was the main corridor into the village.

The humidity, oppressive anywhere in country, seemed to intensify in the canal. Small bamboo dwellings about 50 feet square (affectionately dubbed "hooches" by Americans) lined both banks. Consisting of single large, open living areas, they were surrounded by a bamboo wall that ran halfway up to the thatched roofs, allowing a clear view as well as a cool breeze off the water. The hooches were constructed on platforms that were supported by larger stilt-like bamboo legs and resembled partially-open boxes with roofs.

The bank of the canal crept up at a fairly steep angle from the river underneath the homes. A small gate-like door on the canal side opened to a narrow walkway leading out from the shelters to a series of smaller structures directly above the water. The cubicles, no more than three feet square, perched ten feet or so above the water with obligatory holes in the bottom for nature's call.

As we idled slowly up the canal, I saw that several of these boxes were in use. The occupants—men, women, and children—squatting contentedly and visible from the chest up, waved a cheery greeting to us. Ironically, at the water's edge only slightly to either side of the occupied "boxes," individuals were brushing their teeth, washing their faces, or cleaning the morning's breakfast dishes.

I pointed at the bank and glanced back at one of the crew, who didn't seem the least bit fazed or interested. Realizing my mouth was open in astonishment, I wisely decided to keep silent. I had, after all, already signaled my "new-guy" ignorance on more than one occasion that morning.

The canal was teeming with traffic, small boats hugging the banks. Some seemed no more than slightly concave two-by-twelve boards, their occupant standing in the back, balancing precariously as they propelled the boats forward with a paddle or a long pole. Some, only a bit larger, were powered by small engines with long propeller shafts extending out into the water. They whined with a loud pitch as their operator maneuvered the direction of the shaft, steering the boats expertly in and out of traffic.

A few larger sampan-style vessels ferrying cargo slipped slowly past

Cargo junk on a canal off the Mekong.

us on the way out to the Mekong. These boats were graceful in appearance, some with cabin-like structures on the aft deck for the families of the owner/operators. The families, as was the custom, ranged in age from great-grandmothers and grandfathers so aged that they were hardly able to stand, to newborns, completely unable to stand.

The thought struck me that many of the oldest in these families had never lived a day of their lives out of earshot of gunfire or explosions in this war-torn country. For me as well, the sounds of war would soon be common enough, so that the absence of it would have been a shock to the system.

I was deposited unceremoniously at the main pier for Sadec PBR (Patrol Boat/River, in the vernacular of the United States Navy), my newfound friends barely acknowledging me as they turned and headed back out toward the river. The rectangular-shaped pier, bobbing up and down with the waves, had a repair shack on one end and a dozen boats tied alongside. Buoyed by several huge rubber floatation devices, it had one fueling point on the far corner.

Several rolls of concertina wire funneled traffic in or out of the pier area on a narrow driveway toward a dusty dirt road, only slightly wider. A single Marine guard standing watch at the end of the drive, sheltered from the hot sun by a thatched bamboo cover, waved me over.

1. First Breath

"Gotta sign in," he said, holding a clipboard high in the air.

"What?" I replied.

"Grab your shit and head over here," he answered, somewhat annoyed at having to repeat himself. "Truck's on the way. Ya gotta sign in here."

As if on cue, an old U.S. Navy gray pickup swerved around the corner, skidding to a stop in front of the guard shack and sending a cloud of dust into the air.

"Damn you, Miller," the Marine shouted as a kid jumped from the front seat wearing cutoff green fatigues, a dirty t-shirt, and sporting a green camo scarf wrapped around his head. "One of these days I'm just gonna shoot your ass when you come around that corner."

"Yeah, it'd be the only thing you've shot since you got in country," the kid replied as he grabbed my duffel bag and threw it into the bed of the truck.

"Hop in the back," he said to me, slinging his thumb over his shoulder in the direction of the truck bed. "Hell of a lot cooler back there."

A ten-minute ride through town brought us to the gate leading into the Sadec RIVDIV (River Division) 513 compound, my home for the foreseeable future. A relatively small compound, it was surrounded by cyclone fencing ten feet high and had a guard tower in all four corners. Four military tents 80 feet long stood side by side to the left of the main entrance. My driver skidded to a stop in front of the first one and leaned out of the window, looking back at me.

"Stow your gear in there," he pointed to the first tent, "and check in at the admin office back in the rear of the compound."

I jumped off the tailgate, grabbed my duffel bag and M14 as the pickup pulled away, and stood looking at the entrance of my new home, the dust settling around me.

Stepping through the door, I saw several bunk beds lining both sides of the tent. A few guys lounging around on the lower bunks talking quietly glanced up momentarily at the new guy standing in the doorway. The sun shone through the screened, open flaps on either side of the tent walls, and a surprisingly pleasant breeze wafted through. Not sure what the protocol was, I scanned the area looking for a bunk that might be unoccupied. I heard Jack before I ever actually laid eyes on him.

"Back here, my friend," came a voice from around the side of a set of bunk beds. Jack stepped around the corner and waved me over to an area about halfway down the row of bunks. "You can take the bottom one. I'm up here."

There was something about his voice and the familiarity with which he instructed me. I can still remember clearly that first day, and the first conversation we had, because of it. I felt like I had known him for a long time. His demeanor was matter-of-fact and pleasant at the same time.

There is an unspoken, subtle, almost unconscious process that takes place when two people meet and eventually become the closest of friends. It's almost like a game, with fairly specific rules and steps that must take place. The process, though mostly subconscious, is orderly and follows a pattern that we humans learn at an early age. At five or six, on our first day at school for instance, we scan our surroundings in a search of those with whom we may bond. A quest of sorts, it is a mandatory search for our new best friend, the one we will eventually come to trust with our deepest secrets, and the one to whom we may turn for emotional boosts when we begin to lose strength.

Initially, the search is a visual one. We spot someone who has a pleasant smile or mild tone of voice. We then move to an examination of likes and dislikes to find common areas of interest. This stage is followed by long periods of discussion, mostly about little things, all the while searching for the connection that will form the basis for what we hope will be eternal friendship.

The day Jack looked my direction and said, "You can take the bottom," our friendship jumped in an instant from step one to "etched in stone."

Wearing street clothes, a pair of jeans, slip-on loafers, and an untucked, short-sleeved Hawaiian shirt, he said incidentally, "Get out of the uniform, throw on some jeans and a T, and let's go get a beer. When we come back, I'll help you stow your gear."

"I want to try out my new camera," he continued, holding up an old Polaroid, the type that produced the small instant pictures approximately three or four inches square.

Five minutes later we were walking out the front gate toward town. I had dropped my bag, dug out a pair of jeans and a pullover shirt from the very bottom, and grabbed my wallet which contained only American money.

"Gotta use 'P' here," Jack warned, referring to the Vietnamese piaster, introduced into Vietnam by the French. "Don't worry. It's on me. You can get it next time."

His use of the term "next time" gave me a sense of being at home there; it was a sense of permanence and a sense of belonging that I desperately needed.

1. First Breath

By the time we'd walked the half-mile to the neighborhood bami-bar, a small outdoor French-style drinking establishment, I knew as much about Jack as if I had known him for years. I knew for instance that he had the perfect family: a mom, dad, younger brother, and two sisters. I knew they were perfect because of the way he described them to me. He didn't tell me they were perfect. He just told me little things about them, and he told me in a way that was not ostentatious or bragging; it was just matter-of-fact. There was no other word to describe the sisters and a brother and mom and dad other than "perfect." It was just that simple.

"You'll meet the guys later," Jack explained as we

I was with Jack (front), sitting in "bami-bar" drinking a beer, less than an hour after we'd met. The beginning of a lifelong brotherhood.

sat down on rickety plastic chairs, at a rickety plastic table set on a dirt floor, under a bamboo thatched roof through which the sun streamed in narrow bands. "David and Billy—best guys in the world."

Somehow, I knew it had to be true, that Billy and David were the best guys in the world, the same way I knew Jack's family was the perfect family, although I had never met them and had, until forty-five minutes before that, never met Jack Anderson. Soon I'd meet and be a part of the extended family which included Bill Fuller, Phil Yocum, Doyle Hensley, Don Rogers and others. We didn't know it at the time, but we would become the kind of friends who years later, following phone calls, would feel incomplete if we didn't end conversations with, "I love ya, brother."

"You number one GI," shouted a young waitress, as she sat two tall, clear glasses of beer on the table.

15

A few odd-shaped cubes of ice swirled around in the otherwise tepid brew as she set the glasses down. Small pieces of sawdust floated on the surface.

Jack didn't bother picking them out of his glass but explained as he noticed me looking a little dumbfounded. "No refrigeration here. They just chip off a couple of pieces of ice from a block that's kept on sawdust in the back. You'll get used to it."

"Lin-lee," he called out to the girl who was turning to leave, who apparently greeted every American with, "You number one GI," and was apparently well known to Jack. "Take a picture of me and Godfrey with my new Polaroid. Godfrey just got here."

"Just look in here," he said pointing to the sight aperture, "and push this button."

As she put the camera to her face and pushed the button, she exclaimed, "Choi oi!" (loosely translated, "I'll be damned!"), as the camera whirred, and a small picture emerged, slowly morphing into an image of me and Jack. Fifty years later, that picture, the first of many, rests on my dresser at home.

2

Bonding:
Rite of Passage

The most important rite of passage in becoming accepted into any group is learning the traditions and rituals. Years after I was blessed to have survived and departed Vietnam, I studied psychology, earning a PhD from Mississippi State University. One of the most interesting studies I had the opportunity to participate in dealt with rituals and traditions.

Becoming part of a team or a group involves the simple but all-important process of learning the rituals and traditions, and ever so slowly, melding into them. The actual rituals are as varied as the groups, of course, but the processes are the same.

There is an initial assumption on the part of group members who have gone before you that because you are new, you don't belong; therefore, you may not partake in the rituals and as such, may not be accepted at all. New members to any group have to prove their worth.

It's difficult to understand how one does this, and in fact, many of the permanent members may not even know what has to be done to prove oneself. It just happens. One day, you're seen as an outsider, and the next, it's as if you've been there all along.

It helps to have a sponsor, someone who vouches for your viability and usefulness to the group. Jack was mine. He introduced me to everyone that was important to him, with an almost imperceptible air of pride in our relationship.

"Hey, Billy," he would say, with a hand on my shoulder as if I were a gift he was bestowing on the group, "this is Godfrey, from Mississippi; damn redneck and a hell of a good guy," or "Davy Taylor, you ol' bastard, come shake hands with Godfrey; he's with us now."

Billy, David Taylor, Phil Yocum, Bill Fuller, Don Rogers, and dozens of others, were all part of an extended family of boys, few over 22, who had migrated through various means and channels, some voluntary and some not, to this strange place where a kid became a man in less than a week and had no idea how it happened. Vietnam for them was a moment in time. If they survived it, it would be the moment that defined them. Now, because of Jack, I was welcomed into the fold.

Vietnam had a strange way of reinforcing a strong sense of right and wrong in a person. Jack, Billy and David and the guys all had a pretty good step up on that, Billy especially. Billy was always the first to step in and defend one of the interpreters when someone would slight them in some way.

"That guy'll save your ass one of these days. Just remember that," he'd point out from time to time.

But if any of us occasionally needed a little help understanding where that thin line was between right and wrong, Vietnam would make it clear.

Looking back after more than fifty years, I still remember how I felt warm and comfortable with these new brothers, and it was all because of Jack. Jack said I was okay, and that ended the conversation. The only thing left at that point was showing me where to eat and where to buy a bottle of beer or a quart of whiskey. I unpacked my gear and began my life with my new family.

The rituals were still there: joining in with everyone whistling that stupid theme song from the TV series *Combat* while we rode in the back of the old pickup to the pier to ready our boats for a patrol; positioning grenades, extra ammo belts, the M72 LAW shoulder fired rockets and various other weapons where you knew exactly how to lay your hands on them as you were being shot at. I still had to learn all of this, but the pressure wasn't there. I didn't have to prove anything, and I knew it; I felt it.

The PBR was one of those iconic pieces of military equipment that was designed and manufactured for one war and one purpose. Although it probably wasn't known at the time, it would have very little practical use after the Vietnam war.

The Boats were manned by four-man crews. A patrol captain and an interpreter shifted back and forth between boats for a total of ten men on every two-boat patrol. Before Tet in 1968, only very rarely would a single boat be assigned a mission.

Since much of the enemy movement in that country, men and equipment, took place on the water, interdiction for that movement occurred on the water. The PBR, a fiberglass boat, was lightweight. At top speed, it had

18

a 4- to 6-inch draft and could, if need be, cruise through rice paddies to access remote canals. Its two powerful diesel engines could be operated independently, allowing the boat to spin on a dime and reverse course instantly, which often came in handy.

The boat was equipped with three 50-caliber weapons, two twin-mounted on the bow, and one aft. The front-mounted weapons, fed from either side by ammo belts loaded with a tracer every four rounds to direct fire more accurately, were easily spun around using the body motion of the front gunner.

The twin-50 operator standing in the "gun tub," a lightly armored well behind and beneath the guns, shifted the direction of fire along a 180-degree rotation. The two weapons, fired simultaneously by depressing a bar that ran across the rear of the mount, were the main armament for the boats. They were capable of laying down a formidable blanket of suppressive fire.

The aft gun had a belt-fed, hand-cranked Honeywell M79 grenade launcher mounted on top of it. Similar to the old Gatling guns, a rotating crank handle fired a M79 grenade, fed from a canvas belt, every half-turn.

Each boat had an M-60 machine gun and several M16s with adequate ammo. Additionally, every patrol carried a couple of boxes of M26 frag grenades as well as an ample supply of "Willie Peter," white phosphorous grenades. If grenades were necessary, however, it usually meant that a firefight had gotten a little out of control.

We mostly used the M26 frags to toss over the side and shock fish for the local fishermen who came alongside. Vietna-

Bill Fuller sitting at front twin-50 mount.

19

mese fishermen kept everything that came out of the water, no matter how small or large. Their shouts of delight as they saw stunned fish floating to the surface always gave us a brief respite from the heat and stress of the day; it was one of the times when humans connected as humans, not combatants.

3

Virginity Patrol: Move Out and Draw Fire

As we loaded and prepped the boat for departure that first morning, I had a sense not of trepidation but of exhilaration. The sun peeking over the horizon, casting unbelievably beautiful hues across the harbor, also signaled the coming heat and humidity, as if to say, "Enjoy this while you can. It won't last long, and I have something challenging in store for you for the rest of the day."

I was smart enough to know that my job that day, and probably the next few days, was to watch and learn. As such, I helped where I knew I could without getting in the way, staying out of the way when I didn't know the routine.

Our two boats, the lead boat with the patrol leader on board out front, cruised slowly through the canal leading out to the Mekong. We moved at a snail's pace so as not to swamp the shallow fishing boats heading out to catch the day's food. Many of the Vietnamese fishermen, standing precariously in the center of their small craft and polling their way toward the fishing grounds, waved enthusiastically.

"Most of these folks are really glad we're here," Don Rogers, a quiet kid from Indiana, said, pointing toward one of the fishermen, "but you can never lose sight of the fact that some of them, and you'll never know which ones, are out here at night, manning NVA (North Vietnamese Army) oversight positions, just waiting for the chance to pop a cap in one of us."

Halfway out of the canal, a few hundred yards from the main river entrance, a surprisingly well-built bridge, 50 feet above the water, spanned the canal. Dozens of kids, some completely naked, stood in the center, waving and laughing as we approached.

"You'll get a kick out of this," Jack said, as he pulled a couple of cans of inedible C-rats from a box.

Brothers in the Mekong Delta

As if prearranged, everyone on the boat tossed at least one can of something into the brown water just below the bridge. Suddenly, every kid on the bridge screamed with delight as they dove into the water and disappeared below the surface. Within seconds they began to surface with the cans in hand, waving them triumphantly and shouting for more.

"They're here every day just waiting for us," Jack laughed. "How the hell they can spot those sinking cans in that water, I'll never know. Radar, huh. They probably don't eat that crap either. The thrill is in the hunt, I guess."

On a routine patrol during the day, we stopped boats and searched them for contraband, as well as checking the identifications of the passengers. Virtually everyone traveled by river, and many of the locals made their living from fishing. Night travel on the river was prohibited. Anyone on the river at night was taken in for questioning and possible long-term detention.

Additionally, every PBR section had at least one SEAL team attached. The elite warrior teams did three to six months in country rotations. We were their delivery and extraction mechanism and provided the mission fire support from the water. We never knew when we'd be called upon to take them into the narrow tributaries off the main river, but it was the night missions that always resulted in a firefight.

On these occasions, we'd move covertly into the designated areas (the PBR could idle almost silently, assuring relatively quiet insertions for the teams), nudging through thick foliage and vines along the canal banks most desirable for SEAL team insertions. The team members, between four and six per operation, would slip off the bow of the boats and disappear into the jungle. We'd then back off, cut our engines, and stand by to provide fire support if needed and extract them upon mission completion.

Soon we'd see and hear the high-pitched staccato of automatic weapon fire, open up ourselves on the prearranged coordinates, and wait for the light signal from the shore. When we spotted it, we'd plow into the banks to pick them up, all the while maintaining a steady blanket of fire around them. As soon as they were aboard, we'd back off and head out into the relative safety of mid-river. We rarely knew what their objective was and knew not to ask.

Jack had finagled a way to have me permanently assigned to his boat. All of us shared the same rank—E4—but Jack commanded a little more respect than the rest of us, even from most of the command staff. I soon learned that he had been wounded before I arrived and refused a trip back home so he could stay with the team. As a result, most folks at the command level respected his choice and sort of deferred to him now and then. It didn't hurt that he was gregarious with an unreservedly infectious personality.

Those first few patrols, I tried hard to keep my mouth shut and watch. There was much to learn, everything from where to position myself at various times of the day to what to wear. Most of the boat captains recognized how uncomfortable and unnecessary the issued uniforms were and, as such, allowed cut-off camo pants, t-shirts, or no shirt at all (depending on if you wanted to work on your tan), and sometimes deck shoes or flip-flops. I even had to learn how to relieve myself while on patrol. Attending to a call of nature was accomplished by hanging your ass off the rear of the boat while it was at high speed. A slight, expert lowering of your butt into the intense spray from the Jacuzzi pumps was a perfect substitute for toilet paper as well.

I also tried hard not to do anything stupid. Luckily my patrol mates had a vested interest in me learning my job and proved patient and positive, aside from a few good-natured jibes now and then. One source was the time I allowed a vital piece of the mechanism for our M-60 machine gun to fly through my hands out into the river.

The M-60 has an incredibly strong spring in its firing mechanism that has to be removed slowly, releasing the tension, when cleaning or conducting maintenance on the weapon. On my second patrol, during a hot quiet day as we drifted in the middle of the river, I was instructed to dismantle, clean, and re-lube the 60.

Intent on demonstrating my prowess at this task—I was, after all, the boat weapons specialist—I entered into idle conversation with one of the guys as I systematically stripped the weapon. Forgetting that the next piece to remove was that strong spring, I released it and watched in total embarrassment as it shot 20 yards out into the middle of the river. I suppose it still today sleeps at the bottom of the Mekong River along with tons of other remnants of the war.

Although I received a bit of good-natured, highly deserved ribbing for rendering the 60 unusable until we returned to base to get another part, I was eventually forgiven. For the next few weeks, I managed to avoid similar mistakes until early one morning as we were cruising through the Sadec canal on the way out for a day patrol.

Several unfortunate incidents converged that day to cast another shroud of doubt over my competency. Operational policy for patrols was to maintain a safety status on the twin 50-calibers up front. A 50-caliber machine gun has to be charged twice before it can be fired. A single charge leaves the weapon in a safe status while still allowing it to be fully operational with only a single charge.

The charging handles on the side of the weapon (our twins were designed so that the side-by-side weapons had opposite charging handles, and the belts were fed on opposite sides) must be pulled back twice to shift a round into the chamber and ready the weapon for firing. As a general rule, for safety purposes, we always charged the weapon once so that if need be, a single pull on the handle slipped a round into the chamber and readied the weapon for use. This could be done fairly quickly in case we were attacked. Once the weapons were fully charged, the single bar-like firing mechanism/trigger running across the back of the twin-mounted weapons could be depressed easily, engaging both weapons simultaneously and laying down a crushing blanket of fire.

Occasionally, we received intelligence that we may be attacked soon after entering the main river, although this intel was usually erroneous. Be that as it may, we always prepared for it, and one of these preparation steps was fully charging the twin 50s.

On this fateful morning, I happened to be manning the guns up front. I loaded and double-charged the weapons, readying them for immediate fire, as we slipped out of the pier area and began the idle-speed cruise toward our patrol sector in the Mekong.

The final unfortunate piece of the puzzle was an early morning sprinkle. Our weapons, especially the 50s when not in use, needed to be protected from rain. To provide this protection, we kept stowed in the bow canvas covers with an elastic band around the edge. In the event of rain, we slipped the cover over the front of the barrels and pulled it back to secure it under the rear of the weapon mount. The elastic band held it in place.

As was the ritual, the guys had pulled the unwanted cans of C-rations from their meal boxes and were preparing to throw them out into the canal for the kids who were, as usual, waiting for the signal so they could dive off the bridge into the water below to retrieve them.

The timing was uncanny. The rain started, a very light sprinkle. I pulled the canvas cover from under the bow, and from my position standing in the 50-caliber mount well, tossed the leading edge of the cover out over the front of the barrels with the intent of pulling it tight back under the rear of the weapon. The cans were tossed; the kids jumped into the water. I threw the cover out toward the leading portion of the barrels, only it didn't reach all the way out and secure itself over the front of the barrels. To remedy this, I leaned forward to slide it a little further out so that it would catch over the front of the barrels, allowing me to pull it tight.

As I did so, my feet slipped on the wet deck under me. I accidentally fell onto the trigger bar, depressing the trigger and firing both fully-loaded weapons directly at the kids in the water in front of the boat.

The wet deck prevented me from regaining my footing, causing me to lean with more force onto the trigger. As I scrambled to regain my footing, the weapons continued to fire, by this time having expended forty or fifty rounds into the water. The kids frantically dove further under the water or swam as fast as they could for shore, all the while screaming various forms of "Dinkydow, American!" (loosely translated, "Crazy, fucking American").

The good Lord kept his hand on me and the kids that morning. God loves Buddhist kids too, fortunately for me and them. I've always thought this was probably because I wasn't very smart. Most preachers, I've heard, believe God is particularly fond of those who "aren't very keen." Regardless, His mercy was showered on me and the kids in the water that day. In spite of myself, I didn't kill any kids diving for unwanted cans of C-rations. The incident did signal the end of the ritual for quite a while, however.

4.

THE WIDE END
OF THE FUNNEL

Our journey to Vietnam, to begin a twelve-month or more tour of duty, started weeks before we ever set foot in country. Jack, Billy, and David had met in southern California as they began their preparatory training. They came from various ships and shore stations, each on orders go to Vietnam to serve on PBRs. Because they completed their training and arrived in Vietnam together, they were also slated to return to the States together.

PBR training began in San Diego, California, with a standard country briefing which included everything from the religion to the climate to the social makeup. We were buoyed by the knowledge that only 99 percent of the reptilian community in the jungles of Vietnam could kill you simply by looking in your direction. The other one percent was fairly innocuous.

This basic orientation training in which we learned very little about how the war got started and how America became involved occupied the first three days of our prep. It wasn't important for us to know the ins and outs of the war, and to be honest, being little more than teenagers, few of us would have been interested in the political backdrop.

This short introduction was followed by three weeks of Vietnamese language training, during which most of us learned that there was no way in hell we would ever be able to speak or understand the Vietnamese language. We were supposed to learn how to ask for protection, or for water, food, or medicine, but our particular class spent most of the first week teaching our instructor how and why to say, "Playin' hooky."

The Vietnamese language was difficult for several reasons, specifically because of the voice inflections necessary in the pronunciation of various words. One inflection was a high-pitched tone, one a low-pitched tone, and one began low and ended high, or vice-versa.

Language training was followed by SERE (survival, evasion, resistance, escape) school, right outside of San Diego in the desert. SERE training was, and is, required of any serviceman destined to assignments in which they stand a greater than normal chance of capture. The irony of training in the deserts of southern California to learn how to escape and evade in the jungles of Vietnam was somehow lost on us. Such irony was magnified somewhat by the fact that all of our "captors" were mimicking Russian soldiers. It was all a matter of dotting I's and crossing T's, however, and we understood that.

The most applicable training for us took place following SERE, in northern California. There, we actually operated and trained on the boats in the backwater canals in the vicinity of Mare Island Naval Shipyard in what is now Napa-Sonoma State Wildlife Area. We spent our days familiarizing ourselves with the boats' maneuverability and firepower and took part in exercises with faux Vietnam sampans, learning all the ways we were likely to be killed.

Our last training before setting foot on Vietnamese soil would take place in the Philippine jungles outside Clark Air Force Base. This four-day training was intended to familiarize us with various plants and wildlife we might encounter, including which could be helpful and which could be lethal. We lived in the jungle with native guides in bamboo shelters that we constructed, living off the things we caught. It was here I had my first and last taste of bat. I can only describe it as tasting a lot like bat.

Going through these last days of training in the States before joining the war effort, we all went through a lot of changes, some good and some not so good. This is easiest understood if you can put yourself in the mindset we occupied.

We were, of course, following closely any news from Vietnam, even if we'd never taken much of an interest prior to that point. Some of us didn't even know how to locate the country on a map. We were like most kids at that age, more interested in desires of the flesh and the age-old, late-teen/early-adult quest to partake in each and every vice currently known to man. Only we were a little more motivated in our mission due to the constant reminder on the nightly news of the increasing numbers of our predecessors who were coming home in bags. As such, toward the end of our training, most of us were ready to metaphorically skip school for the last few days we had left in the States. After all, we figured, the worst they could do was send us to Vietnam.

In those days, with the draft and compulsory military service in full force, the idea of failure to obey an order, or even being late for an assignment or a required formation, was virtually unheard of. Additionally, being from the South, the tradition of military service and commitment to duty was an accepted part of growing into manhood. This attitude was reinforced by the assumption that Vietnam was our generation's war, and in the South, we embraced that in the same way our fathers had embraced World War II and Korea. These subtle, cultural "facts of life" in the South combined to create an environment in which most young men knew that they would join the military, obey to the letter all orders, and serve honorably. Disobeying even the most innocuous order just never occurred to any of us, *until* those last days.

After we had finished our training in northern California, we were due for imminent departure to Clark AFB in the Philippines for four days of jungle survival training. After that final stage of preparation, we would, at last, arrive in Vietnam. It was at that point that a strange phenomenon occurred, a phenomenon that affected even us diehard, committed Southerners. We began to imagine bad things.

It wasn't hard to do since there was very little news of celebratory returns from Vietnam. In the days leading up to our departure, Walter Cronkite, et al., bombarded America with pictures of body bags and were, in general, pretty pessimistic about the chances of young men returning home intact. We began to imagine the sexual encounters we'd never have, and the beer and whiskey and wild nights on the town we'd miss. This fear was magnified when you consider that most of us weren't quite 21 and therefore prohibited in the States from drinking in a bar or purchasing liquor.

Going to bed early so we could show up for a pre-dawn accountability formation just lost some of its glamour. Concern over the consequences of disobeying orders carried a little less weight too. It was in just such an atmosphere that Jack and David, two of the South's finest, left a bar early the night before one of the last pre-dawn formations just so they could get to bed and wouldn't be late. Stepping out of the bar, they were accosted by a couple of young ladies in a red convertible and invited for a spin around town. This spin lasted a couple of hours and eventually led to one of the aforementioned, "potentially missed out upon sexual encounters." Bottom line: they were late for formation.

"You guys are due to fly out this morning," the Marine Gunnery Sergeant barked as they stood at a slightly unsteady state of attention in front of his desk the next morning.

4. The Wide End of the Funnel

"Keep this record of your write-up and make sure you pass it along to your command staff when you arrive at your posting in Vietnam," he continued, handing them a sealed envelope.

"Aye-aye," they responded in unison, as they wheeled and left the office.

Outside the door and on their way to the barracks to grab their gear for departure, they were apparently struck by the same thought. The sealed envelope was unceremoniously deposited in a receptacle (euphemistically called a "shitcan") just outside the office door. They did manage to stifle their laughter, however, until they got out of earshot.

As a postscript, two weeks after they arrived at Sadec, the two of them were called into the base commander's office early one morning.

"What the hell is this, Taylor?" he asked, holding up an envelope, bearing the same marks it had two weeks prior, apparently having been fished from the receptacle by a wise Gunnery Sergeant.

Eyes widening, David glanced at Jack standing beside him, the two of them managing a couple of stuttered, incoherent responses.

"Never mind," the somewhat bemused officer responded, once he realized that an explanation was not forthcoming. "I'll contact the Gunny and advise him the situation has been handled. If I were you though, I'd say a little prayer that he doesn't show up here any time soon. I kinda doubt he appreciated having to fish this out of the shitcan."

5

KINDERGARTEN

In many ways, Vietnam served as a sort of ramped-up kindergarten of life. Our average age was 19. The average age of those killed was around 20. At 19, back home in a somewhat normal environment, young men were still learning about life, and the majority of those lessons had to do with interpersonal relationships.

At home, we would be learning how to weave ourselves into the fabric of humankind. We would be learning how to deal with intricate social issues; how to make ourselves appealing to others; how to meet the needs of others while still achieving our own personal goals; and for that matter, even determining what our own goals were. Many experts believe these lessons are the most important a human being ever learns.

The incubator within which those lessons are learned is, in most cases, one's hometown or college environment, maybe a local church, or the guys and gals one hangs around with at the ball game. The important thing for the average young person, however, is that the environment is fairly innocuous and calm. It is a perfect place to grow, make mistakes and learn from those mistakes, and achieve success in relationships. It's also the place where one becomes able to recognize how those successes were achieved and why those mistakes were made and how to avoid them in the future. Of utmost importance during this period of growth and development is the stability of the environment coupled with the fact that no one is trying to kill you.

Our incubator was Vietnam. Our learning environment was a little more high stakes, in that while we were learning all these things, we simultaneously learning how to survive. I'm not talking about the sort of surviving that involves knowing which bus to catch to get to class on time, or knowing how to part your hair just so, or what kind of shirt to wear at certain events. We were learning the survival that taught you how to avoid being shot at any moment; how to respond to the sight of the mangled body of a human being you may or may not have known personally; how to recognize the sound of a bullet whizzing by your head and estimate how close it came; how to deal with the tragic, brutal loss on Tuesday of someone you were playing cards, drinking beer, and laughing with on Monday night.

These lessons, those dealing with social interactions as well as those related to the war, were both necessary and mandatory. They were available in daily classes one could not skip, a fire we would walk through whether we wanted to or not. Although we may have preferred not to learn these lessons, we had no choice. Our only saving grace was that we weren't learning them alone. We had each other, and though we may not have understood the importance of that at the time, we would one day.

A fairly predictable social metamorphosis takes place when a group of young people finds themselves in a closed-off scenario and begins to interact socially. At first, they see the best parts of each other and anticipate, in exploring similarities and things they have in common, a long and fruitful friendship. Soon, however, especially if they find themselves sitting across the same table at meals every day or staring at the same faces moments after they wake up in the morning, day in and day out, they begin to see the bad habits and frailties and faults we all have. That's when true friendships begin to develop. That's when one's social strengths are tested and maximized.

The irony is, in the environment in which we found ourselves, we were made much stronger and smarter and more caring and knowledgeable than any of our friends back home. It is for this reason that friendships formed in Vietnam, the courage and commitment developed in Vietnam and devotion to God, country, and each other, can rarely be understood by those who have never known them. The life and the experiences we shared bonded us in ways few others can conceive. We became brothers in ways that were, and are, difficult to explain. These men weren't just a person someone once knew, like a high school or college friend. Years later, when we would see each other again, a simple glance or a smile would transmit years of shared fears, victories, laughter, and tears, and none of these bits of communication required a single spoken word. This was the foundation of the bond between us.

When we met, most of us were single, which was good for a number of reasons. Married guys sought out their wives for strength, which is as it should be in the normal order of things. Without wives, we turned to each other for support and for understanding. We understood why one of us was afraid, or angry, or mad, and we responded to bolster each other. Maintaining our individual strengths was as important to us as a group as it was to us singularly. Our married friends turned to their wives for that strength, even though they had to do it through correspondence. And although the wives all wanted to provide that sort of support, they rarely knew how since they had no idea what we were experiencing.

There were many happy times, and we laughed like schoolboys when we could, and at the same ridiculous things school boys laughed at. There were still, at regular intervals, scenes of death and tragedy; there were still fairly predictable moments of sheer terror during which we knew we were not going to survive, moments which saw us staring in disbelief at each other, absentmindedly feeling our extremities to assure ourselves they were all intact and still located where they should have been.

Such events were not uncommon to anyone assigned to a combat role; the resulting emotional effects were inescapable. However, the idea that a brother was standing next to you when the smoke cleared, and he understood perfectly the look on your face, was bolstering beyond description.

All of us depended on each other, but some of us formed small, family units made up of brothers as close or closer than actual family members. Sometimes these relationships even resulted in actual, real-world families forming later, when some of us would begin relationships with each other's sisters or cousins. These bonds were strong and developed quickly.

I had joined the United States Navy over a weekend. It began late on a Friday afternoon after I had been given my final grades for my tenth-grade school year. I found myself rejoicing in the fact that I had passed all my classes with D's. I was the second son of a single mother who, although I was still only 17, was more than happy to sign her name allowing Uncle Sam a shot at assuring my continued wellbeing.

Our recruiters' offices were all located in the United States Post Office in downtown Jackson, Mississippi. I realized that if I stayed on for the additional two years of high school, I would probably not be so lucky as to maintain such a high grade-point average. Accordingly, I strode into the hallway of the postal building early that Friday afternoon intent on joining the United States Marine Corps. A note on the door of the Marine recruiter's office advised that he'd be back in an hour. As I was leaving, a big burly USN Chief Petty Officer grabbed me by the arm, assuring me he had a deal I would not want to forgo. I boarded a plane for San Diego two days later.

Like most Southern boys, acting on emotion and an overabundance of misplaced testosterone, I wanted to be a hero. Two years into my enlistment, I volunteered for PBRs in Vietnam. Six months before I was to finish my enlistment, I received orders. I subsequently extended my enlistment in order to serve two tours. Nothing short of God's mercy and grace made it possible for me to be alive to write this book. Every Vietnam vet including Jack, Billy, David, and the guys will attest to the fact that none of us were smart enough to have survived the experience without Him, and His ever-present hand on us. The "why" is still a little murky, but the fact of divine intervention on a daily basis is undeniable.

Interestingly, we all volunteered for service in Vietnam. None of us were wise enough to understand the implications of such actions. In truth, few wars would ever have been fought if young men were wise, and we were, under no circumstances, an exception to that fact.

Phil Yocum was tall with thick, curly hair that seemed to be tangled most of the time and a persistent smile on his face as though he had no idea where he was or what was going on. He volunteered to take the Vietnam orders from a friend who had received the assignment but didn't want to go. Phil was the only one of our motley crew who was married at the time we served in 513. I don't think I ever saw him without that smile, even following the hairiest of firefights. He would often chuckle a bit when the shooting had stopped as if to say, "Damn, can you believe that?"

His demeanor was contagious and always cut through the aftermath, reminding us that as long as none of us were dead or seriously wounded, it just made sense to see the humor in it. He was quiet too. He rarely spoke above a calm tone, even when having to raise his voice loud enough to be heard over the din of the fight. I always felt that he served as a reminder to us that things would get done just as well and just as expediently if we maintained a steady pace of operations. Phil was a source of strength for us, and we all knew it.

Bill Fuller, Don Rogers, and Doyle Hensley were all replicas of Phil. As a matter of fact, we were all action figure dolls in appearance. Like most members of the military throughout history, we were basically indistinguishable from each other at first glance, with similar grooming, uniforms, and even mannerisms.

Bill smiled all the time and had a schoolboy manner, able to discern a joke or a humorous aspect of the most disconcerting event. It was easy enough to see that he did it to ease the tensions for the rest of us more than himself. Doyle Hensley and Don Rogers responded in much the same manner, demonstrating an uncanny level of concern for those around them.

Such altruistic mannerisms may have been a natural response to the

Author (left) and Phil Yocum standing by a Huey Seawolf gunship. At least two Sea Wolves and crew were attached to every river section.

world in which we found ourselves. However, the idea that each of these men, little more than boys at the time, thought about others before themselves, gave comfort, and provided a level of stability in situations and at times when the world seemed to be breaking apart into little bits of surreal impossibilities.

One minute, we'd be sitting on the engine cover over the big twin diesel engines of the boat, cleaning weapons or writing letters while drifting along the back channels off the river, talking about old girlfriends or school days back home, and the next minute, we were returning fire. Once an engagement had broken off, we'd assess the damage. If all our parts were still in place and there were no casualties, we'd be right back on the engine cover, picking up the conversation where it left off. People like Bill and Don and Doyle made that transition an easy one.

Looking back after all of these years, I am constantly amazed at how our late teen/young adult psyche allowed us to tune the war out and involve ourselves deeply into the more important things in life. We found escape in activities such as reading the novel *No Time for Sergeants* out loud or laughing at the antics of Andy Griffith's character, Will Stockdale, in the movie adaption. To think that we could transition from a night in which a firefight had demonstrated to us that debilitating injury or death was always inches or seconds away, to the exact type of conversation one might overhear at a teenage party back home, was nothing short of amazing.

Jack and Billy and especially David were experts at perspective. Jack, a strikingly good-looking young man of 20, always had a story to tell. His stories rang true, with an element of the "possible, if not probable." Most of them revolved around his father, Vance, a man I was later honored to consider my own father following my marriage to Jack's sister, Betty. All Jack had to do was interject, "I remember one time…," and both the war and Vietnam would fade into the background as we listened, a smile already on our lips, in anticipation of a story we knew would make us laugh uproariously.

"Dad and our neighbor Sam Pickens," he began on one occasion, as we all sat around our bunks late one night passing a bottle of Jack Daniels back and forth, having just returned from a night patrol, "had an ongoing friendly competition over who could screw the other out of something."

He took a long pull from the bottle and continued, "Dad had an ol' pig that Mr. Pickens had always wanted to fleece him out of. One day Sam came by and said, 'Vance, I really want that pig. How much?'"

"'I don't know, Sam,' Dad told him. 'Lately, he don't look too good. Don't want you to buy him and be disappointed.'"

"'Hell, he looks okay to me,' Mr. Pickens said."

"Well," Jack continued, snickering, schoolboy style, "Ol' man Pickens bought the pig and took him home. Next day, early in the morning he was banging on Dad's door hollering, 'Damn you, Vance, that pig you sold me's blind as a bat.'"

"'I tried to tell you,' Dad responded, 'that he don't look too good.'"

Jack was gregarious and easy to get close to. When we finally got back home, I always enjoyed going to bars and clubs with him because his good looks attracted girls like sugar attracts ants. He was always sincere in his friendship.

All of us responded to each other in a manner dictated by the clear understanding that our brothers would step into the breach for us if necessary. Insincerity, we all knew, was a game played in an environment you were fairly confident of surviving. Vietnam wasn't such an environment. Insincerity was a game we all chose not to play.

Brothers in the Mekong Delta

Billy was tall and quiet, though you knew he listened to everything you were telling him. As I had grown up in Mississippi, Southern accents seemed the norm rather than the exception, but Billy's drawl was deep and smooth, the way a drawl was meant to sound. He often mixed just the right amount of mild chuckle with it, adding to the richness. His sense of humor and smile were ubiquitous.

I don't mind admitting that I was often scared, but during those times, the guys I hung around most often, Billy, Jack, and David, all had a way and a manner that were reassuring. They seemed to say, without voicing it, "Yeah, man, we're scared too, but there's no use dwelling on it. Everything's gonna be okay in the end, and we're gonna have a hell of a good time while we're waiting."

6

He Was Just Like Me

Memories of Vietnam, for those who survived and returned home, are always tricky. Vets will tell you that memories of even the most significant events are clouded. They're clouded by your emotions at the time they occurred. They're clouded by the recall of others who were with you at the time. They're clouded by how you want them to have unfolded, what you wish was the truth. Rarely are they one hundred percent accurate, with one exception.

I've often been asked over the years if I ever killed anyone in Vietnam. It's an extremely ludicrous question, in that it was virtually impossible to spend a year or more in Vietnam on combat status without killing anyone. Yet I can understand the query, especially when it comes from someone who has no conception of combat in general, and no conception of combat in Vietnam.

Usually, I just change the subject because it isn't really important, and the answer isn't really going to be productive for me or for the person asking. I suppose the act of taking another's life is supposed to be such a life-altering event that others, knowing they'll probably never experience it, just want to understand how killing a person would change you.

In terms of Vietnam memories, however, this is the one exception to the lack of clarity of Vietnam recollections. This one is as clear as a bell. Every Vietnam vet remembers vividly the first time they ever killed someone, up close and personal. I say "up close" because firefights in Vietnam, though close and intense, were shrouded by the jungle and surrounding environment. It's as if every non-human living thing, by design, refused to allow combatants to actually observe the carnage they inflicted on each other.

"I'll provide you an environment within which you can end each other's lives," the jungle seemed to say, "but I won't allow you to watch it. That, I will reserve for myself."

It was as if we were fighting the jungle itself. That single initial explosion from a B40 rocket would happen out of the blue, and all of a sudden, the trees and the jungle would erupt in sound and fury, releasing waves of carnage in all directions. The automatic weapons fire would be accentuated by evenly spaced tracer rounds, usually every fourth or fifth round, but you very rarely saw the guys pulling the triggers. You'd just jump into high gear and lay down all the suppressing fire you could, seemingly on the jungle. Afterwards, we'd go in and try to get a body count, but the North Vietnamese Army regulars (NVA) and the Viet Cong (VC) were masters at removing casualties from the area.

We just never saw anyone. We were given the escape, if we chose to believe it, that we personally never actually killed anyone; we just fired thousands and thousands of rounds into the foliage, and no one was ever hit by a round that we personally fired. You didn't really believe that, but it was there for you.

"You know," Jack once told me, "in the old days of firing squads, I've heard that the routine was always that one person was given a weapon with a blank round and everyone else was given weapons loaded with live rounds. That way you could always believe you had the blank round; that you personally, didn't take another's life."

"Don't know what the big deal was, though," he added with an air of manly indifference. "I mean, it wouldn't make sense here, right? We're doing it. Might as well see it too."

I knew at the time he didn't mean it. Jack wasn't a killer. Unlike many of the young guys over there who wanted to believe they were killers, he didn't even *want* to believe he was one. All of us, Jack, Billy, David, Phil, Don, Bill Fuller, and Doyle, were always ready to step up on a moment's notice. However, in all the time I'd known them, I never heard one of them brag about killing anyone. It was just the opposite. When any of us actually was involved in a fight, it was understood that the rest of us would be available to listen because we knew it wasn't a pleasant experience. Aside from the fact that it took some time to come down from the fear and hype, to come down from the adrenaline coursing through your body, these were kids who still vividly remembered their lessons from the pulpit. Most of us, being from the South, were well aware of those lessons too.

Now and then, though, the routine was upset. The curtain was lifted, and the jungle showed you what it saw every day. You actually saw the effects of a foreign object tearing through human flesh, and you realized it was nothing like a movie fantasy. Occasionally you actually witnessed the very last breath of air leaving a human being and the accompanying blankness, and nothingness, that remained.

For a kid, this was the most impactful visual memory of the war. Most of us had come from environments that stressed the sanctity and spiritual worth of human life. We'd learned growing up, even if subtly, that life begins as a miracle and is firmly in the hands of God from that point on. The incongruity of that miraculous life being, in an instant, reduced to a pile of often unrecognizable waste, was at that time, and would be throughout the remainder of our years, unforgettable. That image would be the vivid, specific memory we would carry with us, the one we'd never have trouble recalling in full clarity and detail.

For most of us, it wouldn't be a memory that haunted. It wouldn't bring horror, dread, and sleepless nights. It would be more of a memory of a brother with whom you were really close, even if you'd never met, even if he was an enemy. The closeness resulted from the shared experience of combat and death.

For me, such a memory was formed on a fairly quiet day just before noon. I still see him today, but he doesn't hate me. We've even given each other a name, although it isn't one we share with others. It just helps us maintain a level of intimacy. We share a life experience, and that experience has bound us.

Throughout the south, the VC would occasionally claim territory, as if they were intent on colonizing it or establishing a small government. Such was not the norm. It almost certainly wasn't an act that was directed from command level, since the guerrilla tactics of the VC were characterized by clandestine hit and retreat type operations, typical of guerrilla warfare the world over.

When it happened however, one telltale, almost challenging action was the hoisting of the VC flag, a star in the middle of a red, or occasionally red and blue, background. The flag would be raised in the middle of a village or on the outskirts of town, signifying that the VC was in control of that area. In the south, such an action brought an almost immediate response from American or South Vietnamese forces.

On this day, we had received intelligence reports of just such an occurrence at a small village approximately three kilometers off the main river on a canal tributary. The canals off of the river in this area were like coordinated traffic lanes, laid out to facilitate travel or commerce.

This particular village was located three klicks west and about half a klick south. Our intent was to simply scope it out and see if there was any visible activity. Aerial photos taken by one of the Huey Seawolf helicopters assigned to our section the day before verified a VC flag flying over a bridge just off the main canal.

We slipped off the main river and headed west on the canal just before 1100 hours that morning. Our weapons were primed for immediate fire. Any time we got off the river and into the canals, we had to plan on being hit. We were usually not disappointed. PBRs were the most vulnerable, but also the most effective, when operating in the smaller tributaries.

We moved slowly past the smaller canal entrance that led into the village area. The tributary led back south at an almost perfect 90-degree angle from the canal we were on. The canal was approximately 50–75 feet across, just wide enough for us to turn around if we needed to.

We were in the rear boat that day. As we idled against the current past the smaller canal, we could see a makeshift, bamboo walk bridge spanning it, no more than twenty yards in. As reported, right in the center of the slightly arched bridge, a VC flag waved proudly at the top of a crude pole attached to the center bridge railing. The jungle was so thick, the canal and the bridge didn't come into view until we were almost perfectly perpendicular to it.

As was most often the case in situations like this, there was no foot traffic on the bridge or normal boat traffic in the canals. Folks had a tendency to stay inside when the VC were hanging around their village. Such an occurrence almost always signaled something ominous. The villagers were put in a precarious position when the VC moved into an area. If they resisted, they were usually shot by the VC. If they conformed, we assumed they did it willingly.

Our lead boat signaled by hand that we should continue west up the canal. We idled another half klick or so into the canal, keeping a constant eye out for movement. In such tight quarters, away from the main river, no one needed to be reminded to stay alert.

At the time, I was stationed on the aft 50. My weapon was trained toward the south, the direction the smaller canal flowed toward the village. Our patrol captain called and told us to cut engines and drift backward, toward the main river. For lack of a better explanation, our objective in these situations was to "move out and draw fire," determining in the most emphatic manner the presence or absence of VC.

As we drifted slowly backward toward the entrance to the canal where we had spotted the VC flag, the silence was deafening. The mid-day sun had reached its summit, and the heat and humidity, like every day, joined forces to remind us that we were strangers in this country and as such, extremely vulnerable.

I stood behind the fifty-caliber machine gun, sweat rolling off my face in waves, gripping the two wooden handles on the rear of the weapon and caressing the small butterfly-shaped trigger with my thumbs. The muscles in my neck and forearms were tense with anticipation. Now and then, when the pain from the taut muscles in my hands and forearms entered my consciousness, I forced myself to relax my grip on the handles.

With little warning, the entrance to the canal came into view. As we continued to drift toward the main river, the canal length was slowly exposed, and the far edge of the bridge appeared. It was as if we were approaching a three-way traffic intersection shrouded by thick jungle foliage. I found myself straining to see what might be coming toward us.

The VC flag was in the center of the bridge, hanging limp as there was not even a hint of a breeze. It appeared inch by inch, as did my friend. Staring down into the water, hot, bored, and daydreaming like a child, drowsy from the midday heat and humidity, he had no forewarning of our appearance. We just slipped silently upon him.

Even now on hot, humid days, I close my eyes, and I know that what I felt in those moments, the relaxed warmth and drowsiness, is exactly what my friend felt seconds before he looked up and saw me.

He was my age and likely within a few pounds and a few inches of my size. The familiar bamboo hat had been tipped off the back of his head and hung by a string. His black pajama shirt and pants were muddied and wet.

Looking back, informed by years of reflection, I imagine that he was probably one of the younger generation who had joined the VC, possibly out of a sense of teenage rebellion. It was maybe even the same sense of rebellion that compelled me to quit school and join the military early one morning, a few years before that day. He had probably been out on over-watch patrol and was tired and dirty from crawling around in the mud all night. A loosely tied scarf hung around his neck, an AK-47 hung from his shoulder.

As if in slow motion, he raised his head and looked straight at me. As close as we were, I could easily see his eyes widen for a moment, then suddenly take on a look of resignation and sadness. He smiled slightly as if to say, "Okay, you got me. I should have been alert."

It all ended in the short second it took me to slightly depress my thumbs on the butterfly trigger. As if preordained, my weapon was pointing straight at him and needed no motion from me, save the slight depression of my thumbs.

More than eight rounds were sent toward him in less than two seconds. I know this because I can still today distinctly remember that two tracer rounds cut through the thick, hot air. The first round, however, found its mark mid-chest, and my friend flipped backward, arms widespread, off the side of the bridge into the canal. There was no splattering of blood like I had always seen in the movies. There was just my friend, flipping acrobatically off the back of the bridge as if he were showing off for a girlfriend, diving backward into the water for a noon-day swim, his gaze shifting skyward, his arms open. He didn't sink. He just splashed down and laid there, still, floating on his back as the smoke from the barrel drifted in his direction.

Assuming an attack, our boats fired up, spun around 180 degrees and within seconds, headed toward the main river. Before I could ask what had happened, our stern dipped low in the water, the bow rose, and we sped away, followed by our lead boat. In less than a minute, we were back in the middle of the river. We cut our engines and all fell silent. The loudest sound was my raspy breath as I tried to stabilize my breathing and flush the adrenaline out of my system.

The routine following a firefight, was thus: once we were in safe waters, the two boats would move up alongside each other and tie off. We'd cut our engines and drift together. This was a time to ready the boat for the next contact, clearing all the shell casings, checking and reloading, and of course dealing with any damage to the hull.

It was also a time to reflect. This was a much more complicated process, and there was no plan or procedure for it. Most of us would be a little shaky, hyped from the realization that someone had just tried ardently to kill us and a little amazed that they had not been successful. Those who have experienced it will attest in no uncertain terms to the fact that on God's green earth, there is no feeling that can remotely approach that of being shot at by someone who is both capable and purpose-driven.

Following the first real engagement I was involved in, the feeling I had not expected was the sheer exhilaration and almost opiate-like high it produced. The high was there every time, and unlike the effects of a drug, never diminished in intensity. That addictive quality was also a factor that caused many young men who had been fortunate to survive their first tour in Vietnam to return over and over again, unable to adjust to normalcy.

6. He Was Just Like Me

There was no firefight that day, only the few shots, all of which I had fired. The only one "processing" was me.

"You okay, Godfrey?" Jack asked, his hand on my shoulder as I absent-mindedly checked the alignment of the ammo belt leading into the 50. "You did good, you know. That was yours, I guess," he chuckled.

"Mine?" I replied inquisitively, although I knew what he meant.

"You know." He tossed his hand dismissively in the air. "It's a good thing to get that over with so early in your tour," he continued, not bothering to go into detail as to what "that" was, as if verbalizing it might give it more power.

"Makes you feel kinda funky the first time it happens, or the first time you actually see it happen. Anyhow, best not to have to deal with that if you're about to go home or go on R&R or something."

"I guess," I replied, still seeing my friend flying through the air, knowing he was probably still floating in the water.

"Man, I remember the first time I actually saw the guy I was shooting at," Don Rogers said, having overheard our conversation and trying to lighten the tone. "It makes you feel a little weird. One of those visuals," he continued, "that sticks with you for a while, I guess. Good thing about it though is that it kinda replaces the last most prominent visual you had, the one you thought you'd never get rid of. Mine was seeing Mary Ellen Slaughter, back in high school, blow noodles out of her nose when she threw up in math class. Damn! Man, that was bad. Now all I have to put up with is a technicolor replay of a guy I shot once, and that really wasn't all that bad. Shit, now I can see Mary Ellen again."

"Man, you're one crazy son of a bitch," Jack laughed out loud.

I would find out soon enough that there were times in that country that were tailor-made for in-depth conversations about feelings, feelings of sadness or fear or regret. However, these times, the immediate aftermath of action, were to be used to slowly return to a state of normalcy, as normalcy could be defined in Vietnam, by kids like us. Talking about Mary Ellen Slaughter blowing noodles out her nose made you realize that life is the same as it was yesterday, and seeing someone die, someone that you killed, wouldn't change that.

"Damn, man," David Taylor chimed in. "That's embarrassing. How in the hell could you ever live that down? Everybody in high school seeing you throw up and blow noodles out of your nose!"

As we drifted, the adrenaline levels slowly diminished, and thoughts of a young Vietnamese boy flying off the back of a bridge, for now, eased into the recesses of my mind. Now more pressing matters such as "embarrassing moments" took center stage, and we became kids again.

"Okay," Jack asked of no one in particular. "What was the most embarrassing thing that ever happened to you?"

"I can answer that," Phil Yocum giggled as he looked up from a box of C-rations he was rifling through. "My mom once came into my bedroom and caught me playing with myself."

"Hell, that's nothing," Jack quickly added. "Everybody's mom has caught them playing with themselves at one time or another."

"Yeah," Phil said, "but I was twenty years old at the time."

As the boat drifted slowly south, my friend drifted into the realm of memory. I'd pull him back to the forefront often over the coming months. That day, however, I would once again be a kid, not long out of high school, talking about the things kids not long out of high school talk about. That's the way we did it.

7

GHOST PATROL

Experts agree, the Vietnam war was not a well-planned exercise. It was, however, a perfect example of the worst that can happen when politicians—the most selfish of politicians, intent on nothing more than furthering their political careers—are in control. These individuals see such conflicts as opportunities, while the warrior commanders see them as tunnels of fire through which they must lead their men in hopes of exiting the other end, both victorious and with the fewest causalities possible.

While it is true that there probably has never been and never will be a perfectly planned and executed offensive military operation, there are logical, clean conflicts where an objective is clear and pursued with specific precision. Many strategists refer to such operations as having been conducted in a manner that demonstrates "controlled chaos."

In such operations, though confusing at first glance, all the individual pieces fit together like a puzzle. Every cluster of fighting men is a small part of a larger objective, and their efforts are intent on achieving an agreed-upon, coordinated end. In such operations, despite all evidence to the contrary, when the music stops, everyone has a chair. Vietnam was a war in which, once the music finally stopped, no one had a chair.

Vietnam was the antithesis of order and control. Many will remember Francis Ford Coppola's fictional portrayal of the rogue colonel, Walter Kurtz, in *Apocalypse Now* and smile at the absurdity of such a character. Those who were operational in Vietnam and knew the environment are generally surprised that there were so few examples of an actual Kurtz.

Vietnam was a playground for warriors, and they were free to play just about any game they wanted. In a strange, convoluted sort of way, it was fun.

Vietnam historians generally view the conflict in two stages: pre–Tet and post–Tet. Pre-Tet was like a see-saw, a back and forth process designed to set the stage for a final act. Of course, we weren't allowed to see the big picture at the time. As part of that group of individuals charged with implementing the policies of "the gods," we were pretty much like fleas on the ass of a dog; our world consisted of nothing more than a patch of smelly dog hair.

When asked what we were doing there, most of us would have pulled out some canned response such as "helping the people do this or that" or "stopping the spread of Communism" or some such bullshit. In fact, we all just figured the "back and forth" would go on until both sides got tired and went home.

For the Vietnamese people, however, it was everyday life. Many of them in their young adult years had never lived a day out of earshot of weapons firing or bombs going off. To them, war was as normal as the sun coming up in the morning or the changing of the seasons.

As for us, we just went on patrol, stopped a few boats, and maybe took the occasional suspicious person in for questioning. Now and then we uncovered contraband such as weapons or explosives being transported on the river or canals. Once a week or so, we drifted into unexpected attack zones. We had names for these areas and unless ordered to do so, tried to avoid them.

"Stay-away Straights," a canal system located a few klicks north of Sadec, was a place where we could, with almost certainty, get into a skirmish, euphemistically called a firefight. It wasn't an enemy stronghold or anything like that, or we would have launched a coordinated operation to clear it. It just seemed like an area, mutually agreed upon by us and the VC, as a good place to gather and fight now and then when things got boring.

Yes, pre–Tet was a time when America was still convinced it could win the "hearts and minds" of the Vietnamese. In doing so, we would marginalize the Communists to the point they would simply cease to be a factor, and we could all go home.

Policymakers in D.C. are those ghost-like folks who are always present (at a safe distance and in a safe environment, of course) for every conflict or war. They know nothing of fighting, other than the fact that they want little, physically, to do with it. During the Vietnam War, they sat in their offices and imagined little conditions they could impose upon us. Most of these folks wore suits, played tennis or golf on the weekends, worked for the State Department, and dreamed of being the originator of some scheme or idea that could be foisted upon those of us actually fighting. If they could do this, they may have a future in politics or at least be able to build a reputation as a strategist (or something).

7. Ghost Patrol

To be fair, occasionally a good idea would come out of these folks, maybe one in fifty or so. Most of the time, however, they just came up with plans that accomplished little more than increasing the American casualty numbers. One such program could only have come from a night out on the town in which some little State Department twerp got his boss drunk and said, "Hey boss, what if we yadayadayada?"

No doubt this little twerp was a favorite of his bosses because this idea found its way to Vietnam, and it was determined that the PBR crews were in the best position to implement it. Thus began one of the most bizarre psychological operations (PSYOPS) ever conducted in that conflict. We inundated VC fighting positions, at night, in the darkest parts of the jungles, from the narrowest and least navigable canal systems with recorded ghost stories.

We rotated the function since it was an operation that virtually assured a pretty good firefight. We usually chose the darkest nights for our theatric effects. To understand the desired objective of such an operation, one must understand that with their deep culture of ancestor worship, the Vietnamese people believe strongly that spirits roam the jungles at night.

In the Vietnamese culture, when people die away from home in unnatural, painful, or violent ways, they don't just drift off to an uneventful afterlife. They must first be prepared for the next stage. The departed souls need certain things to take with them on their journey. Those who were not prepared for death and didn't have their "certain things" close at hand at the time of their death are doomed to wander throughout the night stealing the things they need. If one of those things happens to be a head or an arm or a leg, there are few sources they have to replace them. The Vietcong, enemy soldiers charged with night watches or night operations, were always conscious of this fact.

The "Ghost Patrols," as we fondly called them, were undertaken to induce enemy soldiers to take part in another innocuous, but many agree ill-fated, State Department fiasco: Chieu Hoi.

Chieu Hoi (literal translation *Open Arms*) was the most expensive PSYOPS program ever initiated in Vietnam. In essence, it was a "Come on home and join the good guys. All is forgiven" initiative. Enemy soldiers who were interested in taking part simply presented themselves to any American compound or outpost, held their hands in the air and shouted, "Chieu Hoi."

Following brief processing and minimal interrogation—harsh interrogation was discouraged so as not to discourage others—they would be taken to a minimally secure facility, usually with clean sheets on the cots, three hot meals, and a few cold beers each day. Some facilities, eager to develop a reputation as successfully run operations, even offered prostitutes on a regular basis.

On paper, it looked like a highly successful program. Of course, the "enemy body count" program initiated by General Westmoreland on paper looked highly successful as well. The very best measure of Chieu Hoi success, however, came from us. Those closest to a process always know whether it's working or not, and from our vantage point, Chieu Hoi was definitely in the "not" category.

The divergence between the ultimate objective and the actual process was easily observable, but as is often the case, folks who envision such programs are normally not eager to look closely for failures. In order to encourage participation in Chieu Hoi, it had to be an inviting process, thus the lack of security in the holding facilities, and the optimal living arrangements.

The VC soon realized that Chieu Hoi was a ready-made R&R program for them. Those who had been living in the densest parts of the jungle or in tunnels for months, subsisting on a spoonful of rice and rat meat every day, could simply go Chieu Hoi now and then. They would stay for a couple of weeks, eating and relaxing, then slip off through the lax security, back to their units, rested and ready to go back to war.

Our Ghost Patrols were designed to encourage participation in Chieu Hoi, and on occasion, they worked. On each patrol, we could usually count on a few Chieu Hoi's and at least one damn good, kick-ass firefight.

"What is this?" I asked incredulously one evening as we got to the pier and began patrol-prep.

Two three-foot-tall speakers—the kind 1940s-era politicians would put on top of their cars or in the backs of pickups as they campaigned through small towns—and a large reel-to-reel tape recorder were being loaded and tied down on the rear deck of our boat.

"You're gonna love this shit," David Taylor sneered, waving his hands at the side of his face and mouthing an "Ooohhhhhhh."

"Best chance yet for you to get your ass shot off too," Jack added with a chuckle.

"Yeah, ain't this a bitch. Damn Ghost Patrol, and Jack on crew," Bill Fuller chimed in, drawing the "and" out as long as he could, for emphasis. "If we make it through this night, we will have definitely been blessed."

"Damn sure ain't gonna be boring though," Jack added.

"You love me and you know it. Gimme a hug," Jack laughed, reaching out for Bill, arms widespread.

Bill scrambled to avoid him, tripping over the engine covers as everyone cheered him on with shouts of "Get him Jack," and "Give him a kiss, Bill. You know you love it."

This good-natured charade changed the late evening patrol prep atmosphere from ominous to schoolyard, but the effect was short-lived. Soon we had prepped the boat and run a few inches of tape through the player to test sound levels.

The recorded story, told by a Vietnamese narrator who must have been a professional based on the appropriate voice inflections and drawn out words, was replete with ghostly music that would have caused a chill to run up the spine of the most hardened horror movie aficionado.

Soon we began the slow cruise out of the sheltered base area into the night to what I expected would be the most challenging patrol I had taken part in to that point. We didn't understand it at that time, but reflecting back, years later, I can remember the distinct tightness in my gut each time we left the pier and headed toward the river. That tightness was much more acute during the Ghost Patrols.

Our assigned interpreter that day was a young ARVN (Army of the Republic of Vietnam) soldier, affectionately dubbed "Cowboy" because of the telltale Western hat he wore, and because Americans were incapable of correctly pronouncing Vietnamese names.

As familiarity breeds contempt, Americans who had been in country for some period often developed a disdain for Vietnamese soldiers, falsely assuming they were cowardly. The simple fact was, however, we were going to be there for a year or two then rotate back home if we survived. They were going to be there forever. Our nine lives had only to last for that period. For the ARVN, such was not the case.

Being the relatively new guy, I hadn't developed the anti–ARVN bias yet. Accordingly, Cowboy preferred to hang around and converse with me. The fact is, I never got tired of talking to him and the other ARVN soldiers assigned to our section.

"Tell me about the story," I asked him as we cruised through the Sadec canal.

"Oh, very scary," he responded, drawing out the "ohhhhh" and emphasizing with gestures. "Young VC soldier gets killed many months ago. He can 'no' get to Nibbana, because he lose his head when he is killed. He must roam the earth every night until he find another head."

I knew that in Buddhism, Nibbana is sort of like the ultimate happiness after a series of deaths and reincarnations.

"He roam the jungle every night looking for just the right head to replace his so he can move on," Cowboy continued, becoming animated now and obviously enjoying enlightening me.

"He find head he like," he continued ominously, making an alarmingly effective cutting noise, accentuating it with a slow, slicing motion across his own throat. "Very scary."

The fact that Cowboy never even hinted at disbelief in telling me the story explained why every Ghost Patrol wound up in a firefight. With that realization, I looked around and made sure my armored vest was close at hand.

The Ghost Patrol ended that night around 0500, the same way it ended every other time we did it. Two or three VC soldiers out on lonely hide-sights or night patrols, within earshot of the guy looking for his head, made their way to a Chieu Hoi location and turned themselves in. Along about 0500, we were seriously lit up by some folks who weren't interested in being reminded of the spirits who roam the Vietnam jungle at night. Luckily no one was hit, but it was a timely signal to count our luck and end the patrol.

8

A New Normal

We all incorporated "Vietnam" and our individual Vietnam experiences in our own way. Most of us were young guys, many from small towns, having grown up in a time when the worst violence in our lives was a fistfight if we had seen any violence at all. Death was much more likely to have been experienced at funeral parlors, in quiet rooms with soft music playing.

Moving from that environment to the chaos and brutality of Vietnam was a shock for us. There was no way to rationalize it, but there had to be a process for absorbing it emotionally, and such a process was not taught. Some of us acted tough, as though it was something we had seen every day growing up. Some of us joked about it and made light of it. Though cruel in so many ways, the laughter was necessary to minimize the humanness of the enemy.

We had to be able to see our adversary as something less than us in order to kill him and not "feel." We would say things like "How can these people live like that" or "They couldn't possibly care anything about each other" or "It's okay because most of them want to die and be reincarnated as something better, man, you know; they really believe that shit."

Collateral damage is a term I first heard in Vietnam. It refers to an innocent who was killed accidentally. When that happened, the family would bring the body to the nearest American installation or approach one of our boats on the river with the deceased. Even though there had been a death, it was normal to see a distinct lack of emotion.

At times like these, there was a process in place whereby we would compensate the family financially. Though the actions were understandable looking at it through their eyes, to us it seemed crass and almost primitive. The idea that a father who had just lost a son would take a few dollars and simply disappear added fuel to the fire and reinforced the viewpoint that the Vietnamese people themselves were less than human.

Brothers in the Mekong Delta

"How the hell can they do that?" someone would ask rhetorically.

"You don't understand," Jack or Billy would respond. I was fortunate to have friends like them and David and the rest of the guys, wise beyond their years and willing to swim against the tide in such matters.

"These people have known nothing but violence most of their lives. You can't measure their reactions by your own or against the way folks back home would react. It's a different world here. 'Walk in the shoes' has a whole new meaning here."

We knew it was all a charade. Down deep, we knew that a serious game was being played, and we just had to understand it as best we could for the time we were there. If we survived, we could go back home and back to normal—so we thought at the time. If we could just put it away for now, and do what we had to do, there would be a time much later to understand. Often, we just didn't think at all. Uncle Sam made sure there was plenty of beer and whiskey in order to facilitate this memory loss. Furthermore, the drug use was winked at for the most part, some believed precisely for this reason.

I could almost understand it, but even today I cannot forgive those in Washington, those in charge of prosecuting this war, for putting those of us who were little more than adolescents at the time in a zoo of their own creation. I cannot forgive them for then turning their backs on the youngest and least prepared when those boys lost it and reacted like animals.

A few of the guys had been in country for multiple tours. The obligatory tour in country, unless you were SEAL team members (spec ops folks did their own thing), was 12 months, with a single five-day R&R in one of a number of locations, including Hong Kong, Hawaii, Manila, Australia, and of course, home if one chose. You could, however, volunteer for additional tours in six-month increments, in which case you got an extra 30-day R&R and a mathematical reduction in your chances of survival throughout the next six months in country. It was a serious gamble that a surprising number of us chose to take.

Folks who chose to do additional tours did so for a couple of reasons. It was easy to save money, and the combat pay added up over time. A single, extra six-month tour provided a nice little nest egg, assuming you were fortunate enough to survive. It was enough to put a hefty down payment on that new Corvette or a fancy Ford pickup.

Besides, the 30-day R&R was a huge enticement in that you could pick your location virtually anywhere in the world. The military flew you there and back and, in many cases, provided a little extra pay for spending money.

Guys coming back from France or Belgium, for instance, told unbelievable stories. The fact that most of those stories were probably lies was well known, but we chose to believe them anyhow.

Then there was the second reason. Some of the guys, having experienced Vietnam, combat, and the associated adrenaline rushes, found that they were incapable of functioning anywhere else. At home, they were what they'd always been: no more and no less. In Vietnam, they were rock stars. In country, especially in the early part of your tour, once you had acclimated yourself to the danger, you wanted to experience as much as possible, as quickly as possible. Vietnam was one big, continuous thriller movie in which you were the star at times and the costar at others. Either way, you were "somebody." We expected something to happen every day and were disappointed when it didn't. Unfortunately for many, we carried that expectation with us when we returned home. Just sitting quietly and allowing time to envelop you could be pure torture the first weeks back home.

Folks back home couldn't understand how or why "brother Joey," who'd always been such a nice gentlemanly boy, came back from Vietnam an angry person who often got into meaningless arguments and fistfights. They didn't know, for instance, that the sensation of a split lip or black eye somehow made Joey feel alive and worthwhile, while sitting quietly and just thinking made him feel worthless.

In country, especially in the early days, we often hated to fall asleep at night for fear we'd miss something. That's where the whiskey and beer came in.

At home in America, life was complicated. In Vietnam, everything was simple. People on both sides of the war had roles, and everyone knew what those clearly structured, well-defined roles were. In Vietnam, our imperfections no longer existed. We could use drugs and not be condemned as a drug user. We could be a violent person and not be condemned for being violent. These freedoms were euphoric to many, and the idea of giving them up to go home and simply be that which you always were was unthinkable.

For many of us, once we returned home, we were like children dropped off at the park by our parents and told to "go have fun." All we could do was stand there and ask, "What do I do now?"

In the short time we were in Nam, the lessons came fast and furious, and we grew to know "war and combat." We became accustomed to the constant excitement of knowing we were always being watched from behind the jungle curtain. We were playing this game of "hide and seek" for the highest of stakes. Many of us simply lost all conception of normal in Vietnam. There was a "normal" but it was a "Vietnam normal" and bore no resemblance to anything back home.

Once back in the States, we often realized that we'd left behind something we loved and hated at the same time. Like a drug we were addicted to, that feeling was something we wanted desperately to recreate but were repulsed by at the same time.

We talked about these things during the many hours of down time in the jungles or on the river, and no one felt the need to filter their thoughts or hide their feelings. The honesty was often brutal, but at the same time, it was refreshing. We knew we were different in many ways and for many reasons, and we knew that folks at home wouldn't, or couldn't, understand it. We had become like the millions of combat veterans in all the wars before. The ubiquitous question "What was it like?" seemed so necessary, but at the same time, it was as if something spoken in a foreign language.

"What is it about us that makes us different, makes us odd?" Jack mused one evening as we drifted in the middle of the river. "Why can't we just be still and quiet? Sometimes I feel really empty inside."

"Yeah," Don Rogers added, gazing off toward the sunset, obviously reaching for something in his thoughts. "I hate it when nothing is happening, but it scares the shit out of me when the curtain rises, and someone shouts 'action.'"

"It's the rush, man," Jack added. "It's like a drug or something, and you begin to go through withdrawals if you can't get it. It promises something more, you know, kinda like something waiting around the corner that's gonna change everything for you."

"Dying," Don added cryptically. "Hell, that's what it is. It's the expectation of death, kinda like waiting by the bed with your bags all packed, just waiting for 'him,' for Death to come through the door."

"We need this shit, man," David Taylor chimed in. "When I was at home a few weeks ago on R&R, my mom fixed this big turkey dinner. After we all ate and sat back and were so full we couldn't eat anymore, all I could think of was, 'Is this all there is?' I'm serious, man. It was like I had a big hole in me. I don't feel that over here. Back stateside, it's like you come to the conclusion that the bottle's empty. Here, it never is. All you got to do is try not to die."

"I don't mind dying for my country," Don added.

"That's cause you ain't smart enough to understand the implications," Jack responded, prompting a roar of laughter from us.

8. A New Normal

Known in part for an uncanny ability to throw out completely super-fluous comments, Bill Fuller wagged his finger and said, "See, you guys and your families, with your girlfriends and wives and crap, get back home and start contemplating all this silly nonsense. Hell, you need to be more like me. I am completely unattached, free as a bird!"

"What the fuck are you talking about?" Jack asked.

Not sure how to respond to make his comment relevant, Bill added, "I'm free, is all I mean. Just saying. Don't need any of that stuff."

"You know," David added, "saying you're free is sort of like saying no one wants anything to do with you."

The ensuing laughter lightened the situation a bit. People like Bill served a vital purpose in Vietnam, and we all knew it. He was the guy who always told jokes that had no punch line and wound up being the only person laughing.

"I think it's sort of like playing a slot machine," I offered. "You always want to see that wheel turn one more time just to see what it will bring. Damn, Las Vegas depends on that attitude."

"Yeah," David said. "But would you still pull the handle if there was a possibility the slot machine would spin to a stop and fire a few rounds at you for your trouble?"

A silence ensued, as we all looked at each other.

At length, following time for contemplation, Jack said, "Hell yeah, I would!"

"Me too, I think," Don added.

"Ha, me too!" I offered, though I'm still, to this day, not sure whether I was serious or just didn't want to be left out.

"Yeah, I guess I would too," David said. "Course, you realize how seriously fucked up that actually is."

9

LEARNING TO BE VIOLENT

Those of us in Section 513 were also good at recognizing the amazing qualities and attributes of the Vietnamese people we encountered every day. Political views aside, these people became our friends. As far as we knew, they were all on our side. However, the connections we made with them and they with us were more like the connections we made with people we came across back in the States.

Humans generally have a hard time accepting the fact that people are pretty much the same the world over; and Americans, because we travel to other countries less frequently, are at a real disadvantage in this regard. Young people born in most other countries, even those with modest means, usually get a passport as soon as they get a birth certificate. Americans are a bit more isolated and a bit less likely to travel as much internationally. As such, when an American is plopped down in a foreign country among a people with whom he is unfamiliar, he is slow to relax. It takes a little longer for him to realize that, other than a difference in appearance, these people are pretty much like the folks he left behind. They're good, bad, fat, skinny, righteous, self-righteous, moral, immoral, and so on.

Jack told me a story once that his dad, Vance, had passed on to him. "A couple was driving through a new town once and spotted an old man sitting by the side of the road. They asked him, 'Mister, we're thinking about moving here. What are the people in this town like?' The old man replied, 'What are the people like in the town where you live now?' The couple replied, 'They're mean and vindictive most of the time.' 'Yeah,' the old man replied. 'That's the way people are here.' Soon another couple passed and asked the same question. 'What are the people like where you live now?' the man asked. 'They're kind and warm all the time.' 'Yeah,' the old man replied. 'That's the way people are here.'"

Once I visited the home of a Vietnamese soldier about my age, and his mother came into the room with a newborn wrapped in a blanket. While we talked, she cooed something to the child in a language I understood, and I was shocked. It wasn't English, and it wasn't Vietnamese. It was the universal language mothers use to converse with their newborns, clear to all and understood best by the child and the mother. In that instant, I saw that she was like mothers back home, and I realized that I didn't have to stretch my imagination to connect with them. It was a subtle realization and probably one that was new to me alone but it meant something to me. From then on, getting into the mind of the folks I met over there, the good and the bad, was a little easier.

From then on I practiced speaking Vietnamese a little with the locals who worked and intermingled with us in Sadec, some on the base and some at the establishments we frequented in town. I've never been adept at picking up another language and found Vietnamese particularly hard because of the vocal inflections you had to use to be understood, but the attempt was a nice diversion for me.

Billy was better at it than the rest of us, which was odd because he was the least interested of any of us in learning it.

"Remember," he often cautioned, more in jest than in an attempt to school me, "the word for 'water' is pretty much the same as the word for 'piss,' just a slight rise in the tone of voice in saying either. Be careful when you ask for a drink of something."

The local characters with whom we intermingled on a regular basis were as colorful as a cast straight out of a John Steinbeck novel. The compound employed a dozen or so in various capacities on a fulltime basis, but there were regulars who came at other times for specific reasons.

The barber, for instance, visited a couple of times a week. We weren't required to adhere to strict grooming standards, but I always looked forward to getting my hair cut by him. He was an elderly man who came to the compound carrying the tools of the trade in a small leather case. The clippers he used were operated manually, so there was no need for electricity. Following a neat trim, he would break out a straight razor and finish the job. Submitting to this phase of the treatment required a leap of faith, or complete ignorance, but I enjoyed it.

Young Vietnamese men are very smooth-skinned. They have no facial hair and no beard. The only growth on their face comes as sporadic hairs, rather than thick beards, and it comes when they begin to age. These hairs are accepted as a sign of age and perhaps wisdom, but they are also seen as a loss of youth and virility.

For this reason—the assumption of accompanying wisdom—the two or three hairs that sprout on random parts of their face as they age are never cut and therefore represent a sort of beard, a beard consisting of half-dozen hairs that may reach six inches.

Hair of any kind on a young man's face is unsightly, thus the straight razor. Once our barber had completed a traditional shave, he would sharpen the razor and slowly stroke it, first across the forehead, then working his way down, just under the eyes, slightly above the cheekbone, then across the nose. Finally, he would clean any sprouts from the lobes of our ears. I couldn't help smiling each time I stepped from the barber's chair, my face now smooth as a baby's butt.

We were pretty poor at pronouncing most of the names of the people we knew there, so it was sort of acceptable for us to use nicknames. In fairness, however, I met very few Vietnamese who could pronounce "Godfrey," so it was a cultural wash.

Of all the locals who worked on the compound, the lady who took care of our tent was probably the most loved, and believe it or not, the most respected. We called all of them "Mamasan," though some were not much older than 30. We were trying in our own way to be respectful, but the fact is, the traditional use of the name Mamasan is reserved for one who runs a brothel. Most of the women who worked on our compound had lost their husbands in the war.

The Mamasan who worked in our tent had lost her husband and a child to the war and obviously had strong feelings. She always seemed genuinely appreciative of our efforts. Although she was only around thirty-five, she seemed old to most of us.

To seventeen and eighteen-year-old boys, however, any woman above the age of 30 who happens to be there when they wake in the morning or evening, depending on their patrol duties, automatically engenders thoughts of "Mom." These are boys far from home and probably a little homesick much of the time. In truth, however, she was far too young to be a mother to any of us.

Mamasan kept the tent clean, made our beds for us, and did our laundry in exchange for a little extra gratuity. She was not a loose woman, but rumors had circulated that she met occasionally with guys at her bamboo thatched hut in town. She was attractive and like most Vietnamese women that age, shapely. Everyone in the tent was protective toward her, and anyone making rude remarks or sexual advances was immediately rebuked by the rest of us.

9. *Learning to Be Violent*

We joked off and on with David since he seemed to be taken with her. We were all good Southern boys and brought up to respect women, so our conversations and interactions with her there on the compound were gentlemanly. David, however, spent a lot of time visiting with her when we had downtime and even brought her a little gift now and then from town.

All that changed late one evening while we were sitting around our little beer shack on the compound having a drink. David walked in and joined us, obviously in a sullen mood. He glanced moodily at Jack across the table.

"What the hell's wrong with you?" Billy asked. "You look like you're pissed about something."

"Nahh," David replied with a disgusted flourish of his hand. "Forget it. It's nothing."

Obviously, that's all he had to say to fire up everyone's curiosity.

"Nope. That ain't gonna work," Billy answered. "Too late for that. What the hell's going on with you?"

"Yeah, man," I added. "What's wrong?"

The following comments were directed toward Jack, though not in anger; his tone was more like disappointment.

"Well," David began haltingly, "y'all gotta promise not to laugh."

"Yeah, sure," we all assured him though we were just waiting for a good story and the right moment to bust out and roll on the floor if it was good enough.

"Mamasan invited me to her place this evening. You know...," he explained, "me and her been sort of talking a lot, and I really like her. I mean, she's pretty, and she's really nice to talk to even though her English ain't that good. I can understand her, and I like talking to her."

"Yeah," Billy answered rolling his hand encouragingly, to get him past the trivia.

"Well fuck, Jack," he blurted out. "When I got to her place, and we started taking our clothes off...."

Here he halted as if looking for the right words.

"Yeah," Jack responded. "What the hell happened?"

"Dammit. She was wearing underpants that had 'JACK ANDERSON' stenciled across the back of them in bold letters," he said, holding his hands up forming a perfect picture-like frame.

The obligatory busting out and rolling on the floor commenced immediately, and as near as I remember, eventually even David joined in.

A group of young kids usually gathered around the rear of our compound which bordered a neighborhood of local homes. They played soccer in a small field there, and we kept them supplied with new balls and some equipment. Occasionally some of the guys would gather in the evening and cheer them on, tossing bags of hard candy over the fence once in a while.

They were exactly like kids all over the world and seemed totally oblivious of the fact that a war was going on. Often, in the short times we spent watching them, we could forget it as well.

One particular kid about sixteen or so stood out among them though. He never played. He was more like a mentor to them, or maybe an on again and off again coach or referee of sorts. He never played because he was crippled. His movements were almost as graceful as a trapeze artist swinging from one bar to another, but he had absolutely no use of one of his legs.

His right leg seemed to have developed with no bone structure. It just hung like a useless piece of human flesh from his hip. The surreal thing about this kid was that the rest of his body resembled a Greek statue or something you would see on the stage of a bodybuilding competition. Every muscle in his body, save the leg, was perfect.

He hopped around on one leg, never using anything to balance. It was as if he were a creature created in exactly that form. He could hop almost as fast as many of his young friends could run, and he could leap effortlessly across the small irrigation/sewage ditches that crisscrossed the area.

He took pride in demonstrating his abilities to us on the other side of the fence, and his demeanor was always one of pleasantness and optimism. In a way, he was the epitome of youth in this war-torn country, symbolizing the will and intent to not only survive, but to celebrate what he had and what he was.

I was completely convinced of this fact when one day, through an interpreter, I asked about his workout routine, wondering how he was able to maintain such an optimum physical condition. I learned that he worked out daily, not in a sophisticated, modernly equipped gym, but with sandbags and empty cans he would fill with rocks. This young man and his determination always came to mind for me in later years when I excused myself from workouts because the gym was too crowded, or too far away, or I was too sore from the previous workout.

10

"WE HAVE TO KNOW WE'RE RIGHT"

PBR forces, sometimes called Riverine Forces, were the cops on the beat. We patrolled the rivers and canals in much the same way a beat cop patrolled the roads and alleyways. Though we weren't interested in traffic safety, we were very much intent on clandestine criminal activity. In a nutshell, our "criminal activity" was anything that assisted or enhanced the fighting abilities of the enemy.

Vietnam had developed as a country whose economy thrived on access to the rivers and canals. People traveled on the rivers and canals to meet Grandma for holiday events. They transported goods to market on the rivers and canals, and many actually lived out their entire lives on sampans that had been built to function as a place of work and a type of mobile home/travel trailer.

North Vietnamese Communist forces were adept at moving large military operations through the jungle, but the ubiquitous, clandestine movement of men and supplies almost always took place on the rivers and canals. Large baskets of rice, burlap bags of homeland grenades and reloaded cartridges, as well as actual weapons were routinely transported by water. Our job was to stop or police this activity as much as possible. We also functioned as fire support from the river in organized operations, missions that went haywire when our ground forces would come under fire, and in special operations, SEAL missions. But policing traffic on the waterways was our bread and butter.

Our work was made a little easier as a result of a countrywide curfew that commenced daily at sundown. No movement on the rivers or canals was allowed after dark. In essence, anyone on the water after dark was considered to be taking part in enemy operations and subject to arrest or being fired upon.

Brothers in the Mekong Delta

During the average day, we used a sort of crude profiling technique to determine which boats to stop for examination or search. Occasionally we would get intelligence or informant data about a particular boat or transport operation. As is the case in almost every military operation in history, locals learned early on how to use this process to their benefit to hamper commercial competitors or simply cause problems for a neighbor they didn't like. Our interpreters were normally pretty good at spotting such subterfuges, but even so, we spent a lot of time chasing rabbits.

The daytime process was fairly standard, and long before I ever arrived in country, the locals had grown accustomed to the drill. One of our patrol boats—the patrols were two-boat operations but one was usually used as over-watch or back-up while the other conducted searches and document checks—would identify a boat for checks and signal to the operator to come alongside. This was done by a hand signal. The Vietnamese signal for someone to come closer was a sort of waving, "up and down" motion with an open hand, accompanied by a shouted "la day." The Vietnamese phrase for "come here" was "den day" or "ra day," but as Americans are prone to do, we changed it to something a little easier for us to say, and the locals just went along with it.

If a boat operator ignored the order to come alongside, the procedure was first to fire a shot or two in the air. In most cases, this simple, fairly innocuous warning worked. Usually a boat operator failed to comply because they didn't know we were specifying them, or maybe they were in a hurry and hoping that we were looking at someone else. During the day there were normally many boats on the river.

If this initial warning didn't work, we'd fire a round or two closer to the boat, assuring that the operator understood that we were calling them. If this didn't work, we would escalate the shots and bring those shots closer to the boat or maybe even the operator.

In fairness, there were few other ways to conduct these searches. The fact was that a percentage of daily traffic on the rivers and canals was nefarious and had to be interdicted. Of course, most clandestine movements took place on the smaller canals rather than the main river, but at some point, a boat had to access the principal traffic ways.

If a boat operator was intent on avoiding our search and contact, they most often took immediate evasive action. In these cases, we were clearly dealing with an adversary, and the "safety was off."

It was such a fragile process, rife with opportunities for mistakes. Over the course of many years, mistakes were made. Additionally, there were occasions when we fired on boats and occupants who weren't really trying to avoid us, but seemed to be. Simple misunderstandings in Vietnam often resulted in the death of innocents. Pulling the trigger was the easy part, especially if the righteousness of such an action was presumed in your mind. Only later, and most often years later, did we bring those incidents back and go through all the psychological gymnastics of establishing that elusive balance we all sought.

"We have to know we're right," Bill Fuller mused on one of our after-action, drunk philosophizing sessions. He'd been ordered to fire on a fleeing sampan that day. The round took out the young man piloting the small craft that had refused to stop for a search. "He just didn't look like he was trying to get away. Maybe he was just being rebellious, like teens all over the world," he continued.

The comment was apt, coming from him. At 19, the cleaning ladies on the compound took pleasure in referring to him as "babysan," usually magnifying the indignation with muffled giggles.

"You just have to buy into it," Billy added, "buy into the message that they're not really human, you know."

Billy was the last person to buy into anything like that. If anyone was going to take up for one of the Vietnamese soldiers or interpreters, it was always Billy. He was right though. Human beings just aren't inherently hardwired to kill other human beings, especially when they have no reason to hate them. Therefore, there has to be a reason in order to get soldiers to behave in such a way.

The old professional warriors didn't need it, but the young guys, the less experienced guys, always did. Unfortunately, wars the world over are fought predominantly by younger, inexperienced guys. They have to have a reason to see the enemy as somehow less than human, and somewhat worthy of death—at least until they too, become older, wiser, and more professional. Once that happens, it's easier to kill someone without hating them, as it is easier for them to kill you without hating you. At that point, it becomes a sort of chess match, devoid of emotion. Until that day, however, you have to hate, and you have to have some semi-feasible reason for such hatred; otherwise it's like killing your nextdoor neighbor—the one that's an asshole, but not quite an asshole worthy of killing—over and over again. Most of us just aren't equipped emotionally to deal with that.

"Think about it," Billy continued. "The Yankees saw us Southerners as inhuman; we both saw the Indians as less than human. The Germans, the Japanese, the Italians; all less than human. It's only later, after everything is over, that you can look back and see the truth."

He reached over and jovially slapped Fuller on the back. "Buck up, man. You didn't do anything wrong. It's just the world we live in now, and I'm pretty sure we won't be the last to be put into such a situation. For now, just remember; you stepped up to the plate, and you and the rest of us are doing the hard things, the things those assholes back home aren't man enough to do. I'm really proud of all of us, and I always will be. We picked up where our fathers and grandfathers left off."

We didn't know it at the time, but once it was over for us, individually we'd all feel a pronounced sense of loss, a loss for something we could not explain. When that time came for us, years later, we were like sibling babies from the same womb who'd been nurtured for a period of time, in the most intense way, then suddenly abandoned by their mother. For a while, once the celebration of returning home had waned and that "normal" life had returned, we'd wander the earth searching for our siblings and trying in vain to recreate that period of nurturing. We were like high school kids who'd become adults and were constantly trying to recreate the glory days.

The mother who'd abandoned us wasn't Vietnam, which is why many who've returned to that country years after the war have failed in their attempt to reconnect. It wasn't even the war in and of itself. "Mother" was the adrenaline that constantly coursed through your system. "Mother" was the euphoric experience of the slight rush of wind and the sound of the faintest zing as a bullet passes really, really close to your head, and knowing, but not really knowing, that you were milliseconds from death. "Mother" was a life lived only by those who'd seen combat and those who knew, to varying degrees, what that entailed.

People who've lived normal lives usually have a hard time understanding why so many of us spend the rest of our lives searching for that "mother" who abandoned us so suddenly and so abruptly. Some experts have speculated that this is because the separation was without fanfare or a fond farewell or formal announcement of an end. We were just there one minute with "mother" and without her the next.

"You know," Jack surmised once when we were sitting on our bunks, having a few of our traditional "end of a patrol" slugs of whiskey and entering that philosophical musing stage of a good drunk, "as much as we may hate this place, and as much as we want to be back home, we're gonna really miss it."

"Yeah, maybe you," David offered with a smirk. "I'd never even been able to point to Vietnam on a map before I came here. Not sure I could find it now, tell you the truth. Nope, I ain't gonna miss it a bit."

"You're wrong, Davy. You're as much a part of this place now as you are that little redneck hole you came from back in North Carolina."

"Humph," David grunted dismissively.

"Your blood was shed here," Jack continued, intent on getting his point across, "and it wasn't from a pinprick of your finger. It was the kinda blood that only those in combat shed."

"Yep," Billy chimed in with that sly grin of his that was always accompanied by slight confusion over whether he was agreeing or ridiculing, "the kinda blood vampires love."

He followed his comment with raised spooky hands and an eerie vampire-inspired "Ooohhhhhhh."

"Maybe not that," Jack continued persistently, "but the kinda blood that comes from a little bit of real pain and a lot of real fear. And that's the kinda blood that seeps into the ground and makes the flowers and trees grow. Yep, like it or not, you're as much a part of this country as if you'd been born here, and leaving it and leaving what it gave you and gives you every day ain't gonna be as easy as you think."

11

JUST COPS
ON THE BEAT

From 1964 to 1975, more than two million Americans fought in Vietnam. Five of those Americans killed were only 16 years old at the time of their deaths. Sixty-one percent of American KIAs were under 21, and 12,000 were under 20.

Most of us couldn't buy a drink in a bar back home. These facts are important in that, as young adults barely out of that "kid" status—some would argue, not yet out of it—we perceived our environment in a manner based on a set of guidelines we grew up with. We had yet to mature to the point that we saw the world as adults, with adult experiences and adult backgrounds.

Growing up in the South was not extremely different from growing up in any other part of the nation, with a couple of exceptions. Southern families, especially prior to the mid–60s, stressed politeness and cordiality. Obviously, there were exceptions, but the way we treated each other, and especially the way young people were taught to treat adults, was inculcated in us and held a level of prominence analogous to the law.

It is safe to say that the vast majority of young people, even those who had been in the military for a period of time, came to Vietnam instinctively embracing those basic, positive human attributes which naturally shun harmful actions toward other human beings. For us, intentional violence wasn't easily embraced.

Vietnam was a shock; it was the epitome of a wake-up call for all of us. We went from opening doors for ladies to pulling the trigger on another person, and the trip between was mere inches, the time it took instantaneous.

To be successful in Vietnam, to do your part in the fight, required an immediate deprogramming and a change in moral standards that those who never experienced it could rarely understand. Some would say that culturally, it was a little more difficult for those of us from the South, but that's arguable. The question at the time, though we hadn't realized it, was, "Can the transformation be reversed?" Can a young man go from one who is unlikely to argue with a stranger one day, to one who can easily slit the throat of that same stranger the next, then back to the former in a blink of an eye? Such is the nature of war, of course, and it was not unique to Vietnam and those who fought there, but it was a profound issue at the time and haunts many today.

Bill Fuller grew up in El Paso, Texas. He was a good student in high school, and upon graduating, joined the military and found himself in Vietnam before he'd celebrated his 18th birthday. He was assigned to 513 and made friends easily. He was not only a good person, but he was the quintessential cordial, polite Southerner and instinctively knew how to interact with the rest of us. Few of us tipped the scales at more than 150 pounds back then, and Bill was no exception.

He had been in country less than a week when he was assigned to a boat crew captained by an older, gruff chief petty officer named Beard. Drifting in the middle of the Mekong one day, Chief Beard instructed Bill to hail a sampan slipping downriver close to the bank for inspection.

Stopping and inspecting traffic on the river was a phased process that normally went no further than phase one. Phase one involved the

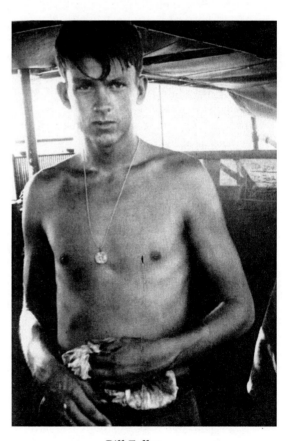

Bill Fuller

waving motion and "den day," usually resulting in immediate compliance in which the craft would alter course, moving toward our boat.

Once alongside, we'd take the necessary steps to assure everyone had appropriate identifications, which they were required by law to have in their possession at all times, and were carrying no contraband. The inspections were completed quickly so folks could get on their way and met with rare resistance since the local populace had long grown accustomed to the process.

Phase two, in case the traffic continued without compliance, involved a shot fired into the air. Once the warning shot was fired, it was rarely ignored. Locals had all heard stories about the PBRs and knew the process was a serious one. If the hailed traffic was indeed taking part in some nefarious activity, at this point they would do one of two things; they'd increase speed or cut sharply toward the bank to get off the river.

Phase three involved a literal "shot across the bow." The trick was to drop a round in the water, close enough to be seen by, but not necessarily close enough to hit, the boat or crew. By this time, it was assumed that the boat was being operated by someone associated with the enemy. If everything went according to plan, there would be no confusion as to what we intended. Of course, any consequences, negative or positive, were up to the occupants of the boat.

On average, it was a fifty-fifty situation in terms of what would happen next. Either the boat operators would figure they had no chance of escaping and turn in our direction, hoping to argue their way out of being taken into custody, or they'd take their chances and make a run for it, hoping to hide in the thick jungle or slip into a nearby canal.

People tried to avoid searches for many reasons, ranging from the obvious illegal activity to the fact that they may have left their ID card at home, which would result in them being taken into custody, if only briefly. Regardless, such an action procedurally led to phase four.

"Take him out," Chief Beard shouted to Bill Fuller.

A small sampan zipping south along the shore had been hailed for search by the crew. Fuller was standing by, M16 in hand, pointed skyward.

"The damn boat was no more than 100 yards or so from us and close enough to see only two folks on board," Bill said, as we sat around drinking a beer at the compound bar that evening.

"Hell, they were way too close to think they could get away. I just figured they thought maybe we'd lose interest or something and let them go, and maybe that was the reason they didn't stop. The damn boat was so small; they couldn't have been smuggling anything important."

"Hell, I just didn't want to shoot the kid," he continued pensively. "Damn Beard was really pissed at me."

"Shoot the son of a bitch," Beard had shouted as Fuller just stood there looking at him in a confused manner, while the escaping boat inched closer and closer to the thick foliage of the shore and freedom.

"He just grabbed my 16, and opened up on them," Bill continued.

"Did he hit 'em?" I asked.

"Popped the boat driver. He's dead," Billy chimed in as Fuller took a deep draw from his beer, obviously not wanting to go into it. "I heard them talking about it earlier. Damn boat capsized, and the passenger swam off and got away. Don't know whether it was carrying anything or not."

"I just couldn't wrap my head around shooting a kid because he wouldn't stop," Bill said. "I know I fucked up, and Beard probably doesn't want me on his boat anymore."

"Fuck Beard," David spoke up without hesitation. "Hasn't been that long ago when he was new to country. He's just gotta remember that. We all go through something like this, and you just need to blow it off."

"Yeah, fuck Beard," Billy agreed.

"Yeah, fuck him." Jack grinned mischievously, recognizing where we were going with this spontaneous moment of levity for Bill.

"Yeah, fuck him," I offered.

We looked at each other, grinning at first, then chuckling slightly, building to a good laugh as David chimed in again for emphasis, "Yeah, fuck him."

Looking back on the entire Vietnam experience, I'm not sure I could have weathered it as well without the humor, understanding, and empathy of those guys. Fuller was experiencing something we had all felt at one time or another; an event, a possible wrong, that can't be righted but can be understood and coped with as long as there were folks like David and Jack and Billy.

Each of us learned in our own way, how to respond to the harshness of war and how to understand, or at least absorb, this new reality to the extent that we ourselves didn't stand out as the "odd man."

The whole world had witnessed a South Vietnamese Chief of National Police, Nguyễn Ngọc Loan, lift a .38 caliber revolver to the head of a handcuffed VC prisoner and casually pull the trigger, killing him instantly. The moment was captured by the Associated Press and NBC news crews, and the film clip circulates still today during related historical footage. The world outside Vietnam saw that footage one way; many of us in Vietnam saw it another. As is always the case, the image was filtered by each of us through the sift of our own perceptions and experiences.

It happened in the streets of Saigon in February of 1968, a month after the Tet offensive. I can't remember exactly what I personally felt when I first saw it or heard about it while still in country. What I can imagine is how I would have seen it and filtered it while sitting in a classroom in high school a couple of years before. The filter through which the scene would have passed in each instance was, and is, vastly different. This, at least, I do know.

As harsh and unfeeling as this may sound, I was in a Vietnam still heavily involved in the aftermath of Tet and associated operations. When I heard that a police chief in Saigon had summarily executed a VC prisoner, I was unmoved. I was a little shocked that he'd chosen to do it on national television, a feeling that was echoed by Jack and David and the guys.

"Guy thinks he's auditioning for a John Wayne movie, huh," was a typical response among us.

As a matter of fact, I remember all of us being a little confused as to the shock it had caused back home.

"Fighting a fuckin' war over here, folks," Jack said. "Damn people expect you to do that without hurtin' anyone's feelings, I guess."

It's safe to say that none of us would have felt that way as high school kids, but at the time, in the moment, we couldn't understand feeling any other way. Soldiers and combat veterans understand that such a metamorphosis is necessary in the pursuit of war. The bending of "who and what you were," into the "who and what you must be now" has to take place to avoid the break. However, once it is underway and that change is slowly taking place, it is surprising how much the human psyche can handle while still allowing a measure of sanity and a measure of humanity.

Early one morning, while the sky was slipping from black to grey twilight on its way to full sunrise, the SEAL team leader for a new team that had just arrived, along with two of his team members, showed up as we were prepping for patrol. With little more than a nod of greeting and acknowledgment by our patrol lead, they jumped on board. As they lacked full operational gear, I knew we weren't going on a mission of any sort.

"Taking them a few klicks north to a Special Forces A-camp for a visit today," Billy said as he jumped from the pier to the boat deck. "Be a hairy day today. The area around that damn A-camp is always hot."

11. Just Cops on the Beat

A couple of hours later, we slipped off the main river, powered down, and moved as quietly as possible into a canal. Two or three sharp bends through the jungle led us to a surprisingly large clearing with several well-kept structures and an unusually sturdy pier, large enough for us to tie off on both sides.

Two unkempt, bearded soldiers, obviously at a command level for the A-camp, were waiting on the pier as we slid alongside and threw our mooring lines to two ARVN soldiers. Our SEALs jumped off the boat and were greeted by first name by the soldiers. Special Ops people, regardless of branch of service, often knew each other, especially among those who'd served in country.

"Might as well chill out for a while," Billy said. "Let's walk around and check things out."

The post was small but well-constructed and circled by the ever-present concertina wire strands, stretched out in accordion fashion and covered in razor-sharp blades. Support team ARVN soldiers called "strikers" lounged in various locations on the compound with several manning machine gun towers twelve feet or so in the air in diagonal corners of the compound.

Our boat captain strolled off with the team leaders to a thatch-covered area, beneath which sat a worn table, similar to a picnic table, in the very center. Billy and I walked around the perimeter trying to find a shady spot.

Special Operations personnel were the first in country, arriving soon after our government had determined that we would be involved in the Vietnam conflict. Euphemistically known as "advisors," their job was to assess the situation before traditional troops were sent in. They also established conclaves among the locals as well as among the established military forces. Unbeknownst to the general public, this process has always been followed in situations where it is likely American troops would be deployed.

In addition to making contacts and forming groups of trusted locals to advise and assist our forces at the right time, they also helped train and equip our allies. They had to be knowledgeable of the local populace and local cultures, how to identify the KLs (key leaders), and how to interact with them in order to maintain close alliances.

Special ops guys were independent and often isolated, fully capable of providing for themselves for lengthy periods of time. They knew exactly how far to go in guiding and interfering with local processes, and knew when to back off and watch the waters flow as they were intended without jumping in and trying to change anything.

Brothers in the Mekong Delta

We rounded a corner strolling toward the back of the compound, the midday heat bearing down as sharp and intense as a pickax pounding into our backs. I noticed a group of four strikers in the shade of a thatched wall, squatting on their haunches the way men of that part of the world did when relaxing, their AKs leaning against the wall behind them. They laughed and pointed at the ground in front of them, and I realized they were playing a type of dice game popular with the ARVNs.

My attention was drawn to a spot behind them. There stood an enclosure, approximately five feet square with a thick, barbed wire matting across the top and around sides that were no more than twelve inches high. Inside that barbed wire enclosure was a young man, legs crossed underneath him, bent over at the waist, blindfolded and with his hands tied behind his back. Though bent over as low as possible, his back was less than an inch away from the sharp points of the wire's barbs in the matting above him.

His back had several deep scratches and cuts where he had apparently raised upward in an attempt to alleviate the pain from his crouched position, indicating he had been in that position for some time. Even more disturbing to my "pre-metamorphosis," "pre–Vietnam," 'high school" nature, was the nonchalant, disinterested nature of the strikers playing the game. Apparently delegated to guard the man, or at least be aware of his position and condition, it was clear that his confinement was of little concern to them.

I looked quizzically at Billy. Billy had been in country longer than I, and had, by extension, been exposed to more and understood more. My look in his direction was actually a question, or rather a series of questions: "Should this be a concern? Should we care? Is this something I should pretend to see and not care about or to ignore altogether? Is it okay with you, and should it be okay with me?"

Billy answered all these queries, first by looking back at me, and second by shrugging his shoulders as if to say, "I don't have the answers you're looking for."

We continued around the other side of the compound and back to the boat. As we passed the covered makeshift table where the meeting was still going on, I was conscious of an urge to mention something about the guy in the barbed wire pen. They were obviously aware of it but seemed oblivious.

"Come on, man," Billy urged me toward the boat as he could see that I was confused.

11. Just Cops on the Beat

We jumped from the pier to the deck and slipped down under the small canvas covering that shielded at least half the deck from the sun. Sitting down and leaning against the fiberglass hull, I grabbed a cup and filled it with chilled water from the cooler we carried onboard.

I sat there quietly for a moment, not mentioning the guy in the pen and hoping my failure to say anything would indicate my maturity toward matters of war. At the same time, however, I was wondering if Billy would say something or simply open a conversation about the latest John Wayne movie or the last letter he got from home.

As I often took my cues from Jack and Billy and David, and would to this day if the occasion warranted, I'd take my cue from Billy on that day. He was quiet about the guy in the pen. As such, the guy slipped into the recesses of my mind, squarely into the category of "things that happen in war," and until our guys came back to the boat to return to Sadec, we did indeed talk about John Wayne's movie *The Green Berets*. We wondered aloud how these SF guys would feel about Wayne's portrayal of them. We didn't wonder aloud what Wayne would say about a small barbed wire enclosure within which a young man lay, hands tied behind him, bent over at the waist in the midday sun.

We were still young and still operating under the direction of our fathers or our mothers or our grandmothers or our preachers or our Sunday school teachers back home. Those directions were simple and clear and had been delivered to us in various ways since we were old enough to understand the simplest forms of communication: treat people with respect; all people deserve a smile or a pat on the back; all people are like you in that they want to be appreciated or treated with dignity. It was the purest form of the Golden Rule.

Those were the directions of the non-combat world, the directions that applied back home. They did not, and could not, apply in Vietnam. A different set of rules and directions applied in Vietnam, as they did in all combat scenarios throughout history. The bad thing was that we only had a few minutes to learn them, and most of them were learned on the fly. These directions were just as valid and meaningful, but they were in total contrast to what we had been taught. It's appropriate to put a young man in a barbed wire enclosure; it's acceptable, and everyone understands it, including the young man in the cage.

Soon I would learn of the atrocities perpetrated on our men who'd been captured by the VC, and I would grow a little more in the process.

Brothers in the Mekong Delta

Whether good or bad, that day contributed to my growth and maturity and my metamorphosis from high school to Vietnam and the new normal I was soon to accept without question. It was through this "new normal" filter that I viewed Chief of National Police Nguyễn Ngọc Loan's execution of the handcuffed VC prisoner.

12

ALL'S WELL IF YOU CAN SEE PAST THE TREES

Most of us younger guys had a hard time seeing the beauty of Vietnam. Recognizing the beauty of a strange land takes a measure of maturity and for the normal teen, we just hadn't reached that point of emotional growth. Our focus was still on the best places to get a cold beer and the best places to meet the prettiest girls. Guys like Billy, however, were different. Easily confused for a 30-year-old, Billy could see it. He saw past the girls and the beer, and even the gunfire and the explosions, and saw a really beautiful country.

"Just look at the way the sun shines through those treetops," he'd comment on occasion as the sunset would filter through the thick jungle, casting finger-like rays of all the colors of the rainbow out onto the river.

"What?" would come the predictable, honestly perplexed response from me or David or Jack.

"Man, it's just a damn jungle and besides, it's hot as hell and there's stuff out there that'll eat you," was often all we could muster in response.

In retrospect, Vietnam was and probably still is one of the most beautiful countries in the world. The war obscured that from most. Young men who lack the maturity of someone like Billy always fail to see the simple beauty in places or people or situations. Then you add to that the fact that Vietnam was first a hostile place. For us, it was a hostile place before it was a beautiful place, and it took maturity to get past that first descriptor.

We did, however, recognize the oddities. There were the things that were in our minds that were specifically "Vietnam," the things that little voice inside us would label, "You ain't gonna see that anywhere else."

Most of these things had a common thread running through them, though I'm not sure I or any of us realized it then. The people of Vietnam had an uncanny ability to look at the simple and see the optimal. A simple discarded beer can could become part of a wall, made of split and flattened beer cans. A young man who envisioned himself a bodybuilder based on a discarded American magazine he'd once seen could see a way to get there, using old, empty cans, each filled with precisely the right amount of water, creating his own little gym. It was easier to see the wonder in these things.

Sitting in an outdoor, French-style bami-bar in downtown Can Tho, Vietnam, with Phil Yocum one day, I was approached by a young boy of ten or so with a bamboo tray containing unopened packs of American cigarettes.

"You buy, mister," he urged.

"GI number one," he continued as we glanced his direction. The perfect sales pitch always contained the ubiquitous "GI number one." Couldn't make a sale without it.

"Sure, what the hell," I responded pulling some coins from my pocket. I grabbed a pack of Kool filters and asked how much.

"Fifty cents, mister," came the swift reply.

"How the hell do these kids ever make any money from this?" I mused as I opened the apparently fresh pack of cigarettes. "I don't know where they get them, but I know they can't get them for less than fifty cents a pack. Seems like a wasted effort to me."

Phil smiled knowingly and said, "Pull all the cigarettes out of the pack and lay them out here on the table."

As I pulled the cigarettes out one by one and laid them side by side, Phil picked a wood chip out of his beer glass and said, "Now count them."

To my amusement, there were exactly 19 cigarettes in the pack, which should have contained 20. I examined the package itself with a look of amused confusion.

"Where in the hell do they get packs of American cigarettes with only 19 in them?"

"They don't," Phil responded, a sly expression of "Gotcha" on his face.

"That's how they make money. If you look really close, you'll see that pack has been opened and resealed. You have to look really close though 'cause they're good at it. They take one cigarette from each of 20 packs. Once they get 19 or maybe 20, they fill an empty pack and seal it and that's their profit."

Taking nothing and making something was common in Vietnam and added to the country's beauty and mystery. We may not have been able to appreciate Billy's "beautiful rays of sunshine coming through the jungle trees," but we could appreciate that.

12. All's Well If You Can See Past the Trees

Walking down another dusty, rutted main street in Vinh Long one day, Jack and I passed a street vendor. The old man had spread a large blanket on the edge of the sidewalk and had all his wares laid out neatly in a semicircle around him. Packages of chewing gum, mints, and cigarettes were mixed in with cookie packs and cheap plastic trinkets.

The man sat perfectly still, cross-legged on the back edge of the blanket. He wasn't hawking his wares. The Vietnamese weren't known for loud or aggressive sales pitches. He just sat there waiting for a customer.

The noon heat and humidity were oppressive, and the flies were thick and extremely annoying. They seem to gather and almost flock in clouds most heavily when the humidity was at its peak, and that day was perfect for them.

Jack stopped and picked up a bracelet made of woven horsehair or something. As he examined the bracelet, the flies swarmed around the center of the blanket directly in front of the old man. I noticed he had an old Gulf spray can beside him, the kind with the long tube atop a container, and a plunger that could be withdrawn and pushed forward, sending a spray of chemicals out into the air.

The man reached very slowly for the can, seeming to conserve his body movements, as virtually nothing moved but his two hands. Jack, intent on the bracelet, didn't notice.

Just as the man picked up the can, I noticed a small wick similar to a candle wick in the very front of the long tube where the chemicals would come out when the plunger was depressed. The wick was lit, a small flame dancing around the tip. He pointed the can toward the swarm of flies and withdrew the plunger slowly. Suddenly he pushed it forward with a swift motion, and a ball of fire ten inches in diameter flared out of the tip, instantly searing a hundred flies at once.

"Son of a bitch!" Jack exclaimed as he dropped the bracelet and jumped back.

For the first time, the man's expression changed, as a slight smile crossed his lips.

"Man, we gotta get one of those," I said. "He must have diesel fuel or something in that spray container. Son of a bitch, what a fly killer."

We learned something new every day about the people of Vietnam. Most of the things we learned engendered respect in us. Individually, we liked them and wanted them to like us. As an occupying force, however, we were not allowed to do that. We couldn't like them because our friends were dying there, and when our friends died, they just went on as though nothing had happened. Because of that, we were required to dislike them, even to an extent to hate them.

I resented having to hate them, or even to dislike them, but at times I did it. I did it because at those "times," the people around me did it, and more than anything I needed to be accepted by the people around me. I used the terms "slope" or "slant eye" or "gook," and I talked of a willingness to "wipe them all out" because that was, at "those times," required. Later, I often felt like a coward.

Around Billy and Jack and David and all the rest of the guys, though, I didn't have to do that. We were a refuge for each other in so many ways, and one of the most powerful was emotional support. I always respected Billy and Jack and David because they were brave, not simply brave in battle, but brave in their individuality. I tried in many ways to be more like them in those days. Sometimes I succeeded and sometimes I didn't, but they were always there for me.

13

SIMPLE LITTLE SPACES
FOR REFLECTION

Throughout South Vietnam, wherever American servicemen were stationed, the United States made sure the liquor flowed. Though an
abundance of beer and whiskey had traditionally been available on military
installations the world over, it was particularly important in Vietnam. Most
of the young men in country were unaccustomed to the things they were
seeing on a regular basis and needed the diversion. Besides, marijuana and
heroin were both readily available on the open market, and the government
hoped that servicemen would choose alcohol instead.

Additionally, many of the young men sent to fight had yet, due to their
age, had the pleasure of sitting down at a bar, even on established military
bases back home, and ordering a drink without using a false ID. This social
opportunity was now openly available to them, and as is the case with most
heretofore forbidden pleasures, many initially abused the privilege. At that
point, those of us prone to addictive behaviors were off and running.

Beer, when not free, could be purchased for a dime. Bottled whiskey
was sold only by the quart and generally went for $2.00. If you were fortu-
nate enough to be stationed close to Saigon, bars and nightclubs, mimicking
in every way those found in any major city in the United States, were open
24 hours a day, seven days a week, replete with the Vietnamese versions of
everyone from Roy Orbison to the Supremes.

Further out, in smaller communities such as Sadec, French-style open,
thatched-roof cafes served warm beer in tall, cheap glasses. The brew, a local
brand euphemistically called Tiger Beer, was cooled by ice chunks chipped
off larger blocks stored in barrels of sawdust to slow the melting.

Picking out a few flecks of sawdust that generally floated to the top of
your drink was a small price to pay for the chance to pretend you were sitting in a café in Paris, even though such took some imagination. The local

girls—often not prostitutes, though the mistake may be made honestly—were glad to just sit and talk with you.

The great thing about our 513 guys was that everyone went out of their way to make life pleasant for the section. One time, Bill Fuller and a couple of the guys went water buffalo hunting in a free-fire zone so the rest of us could have a barbecue. As the water buffalo is not exactly wary game, they were immediately successful. Just as immediately, they were reprimanded, fined the cost of the animal for the farmer who owned it, and confined to their tent while the rest of us enjoyed the resulting cookout.

Jack was good at coming up with ideas to gin up the atmosphere. For example, every small enclave of American servicemen had at least one primitively constructed bar which offered little more than a roof over your head but seemed as opulent as any hometown Dew Drop Inn for homesick kids. Jack and Billy took it upon themselves to construct the one on Sadec's PBR compound. The conversation around the tables in our little drinking establishment often centered on how they'd built it.

"You'd have gotten a kick out of that, Godfrey," Jack began the story, one day shortly after my arrival. He and David and Billy Moore and I were sitting around a table drinking cold Falstaff from cans that had to be opened with old, triangular-shaped openers.

"We needed some lumber, and the only folks anywhere around here who had any were the Marines at another compound about 10 klicks north of us."

He paused there, the three of them holding hands over their mouths and glancing furtively at each other, as kids will do when they're telling a funny story, knowing the end but anxious to draw out the suspense.

"The three of us took the old pickup and drove over there about two in the morning, backed up to their lumber pile and, as quiet as mice," here his voice lowered appropriately, "started loading boards on the truck."

Billy jumped in over protestations from Jack and giggles of support from David. "All of a sudden, this big damn, jarhead with a M16 pointed at us came around the corner shining his flashlight in our direction. 'What the hell are you assholes doing out here?' he yelled at us."

"Yeah, yeah," David chimed in. "As sharp as you please, Jack jumped in and said, 'Sorry man, we were just dumping this wood to get rid of it.'"

By this time, though they'd told the story a hundred times, they were roaring and slapping their knees.

"Son of a bitch," Billy offered for emphasis. "Damn guy yelled at us and said, 'You sonsabitches, load every bit of that crap on that truck and get it the hell out of here!'"

I have to admit, this being the first time I'd heard the story, I couldn't help joining in on the laughter. Jack was like that though. As a matter of fact, they all were, but Jack was spontaneous about it. The "right thing to say" just sort of came out of him, even under the most extreme circumstances.

I made a lot of really close friends in Vietnam but Jack and I were like brothers. It was as though we were meant to have met in that place, at that time. We were so close to Billy and David that the four of us formed an unusual, nuclear family. Though I didn't know it at that time, the relationship would last forever. Bonds formed in Vietnam were like that. (Jack and Billy died years later, within two weeks of each other.)

We patrolled together; we stayed in the same tent; we went to the chow hall, a tent that leaked profusely, together; and we shared many and many a beer or quart of whiskey over tales of home and hopes and aspirations. Our favorite discussions dealt with the dragons we would slay and the dreams we would make come true when we got home.

Being single at the time, we also talked a lot of future wives and children. Though unspoken however, all these conversations had at their base a slight layer of fog within which lay the very real possibility that one or more of us wouldn't make it.

That possibility rose to the surface now and then when someone was killed in a firefight. When that happened, we drank, we mourned, we spoke of the revenge we'd get on those "slimy little slope bastards." We tried desperately to voice our feelings, and above all, we'd talk about the possibility of it happening to one of us.

On September 28, 1967, Joe Musetti and Gilbert Graham were killed. Musetti was 24, and Graham was 21. As with most violent casualties in the war, their deaths came in an instant. One minute they were alive, and the next they were little more than a compilation of all the chemicals and matter that come mysteriously together to form a human being, save the one ingredient most necessary, the soul. From that moment on, they were rarely ever referred to as human beings; they were casualties. Casualties. The term sounded so benign, almost like a mistake or an accident. Best, I suppose, to dehumanize those who lost their lives as quickly as possible so as to begin the mourning process, cycle quickly through it, and return to the task at hand.

Jack had been on the patrol with them and was seriously wounded;

this was one of several incidents in which he was hit but survived. The boat was hit almost simultaneously by three B40 rockets. Two of the rockets impacted within two to three feet of Musetti and Graham. Graham was in the forward fifty-gun position. Musetti was standing at the wheel in the coxswain's position protected by ¼ inch of fiberglass. This is precisely where one of the rockets impacted. Jack was manning the aft 50.

The patrol had entered a small tributary off the main river on a routine patrol. This necessary function of patrolling always put us in jeopardy due to the lack of maneuverability. Boats in the canals were much easier to hit.

One of the rockets ruptured the fuel tanks, which immediately ignited the fiberglass hull. Estimates are that the entire boat was destroyed by fire within minutes. Neither Graham's nor Musetti's body was ever recovered.

Jack stayed with the burning boat, providing cover fire for the remaining crew members as they dove overboard and swam for shore. When they had cleared, he too dove over and though wounded, swam toward shore until the cover boat could pluck him from the canal. His cover fire, investigators concluded, allowed his fellow crew members to make it until they could be picked up. Jack, though he could have gone home, at his request, recovered from his injuries and returned to the unit. He was awarded a Purple Heart and Bronze Star for bravery.

When the remains of the boat were finally recovered, it was determined that the heat was so intense, it warped the fifty caliber machine gun's barrels. Investigators determined that Musetti's and Graham's bodies had likely been completely consumed by the fire.

14

THINGS WE SHOULD HAVE SAID

"It's a damn shame, ain't it," Billy said, as he flicked a piece of sawdust from the foam in his glass of beer.

"Yeah," David added. "I just talked to Joe a day or two ago. Damn great guys, both of them. Can't believe they're gone."

"I mean it's a damn shame that I never told him that I thought he was a hell of a nice guy," Billy said, leaning across the table and waving his hand for emphasis. "Damn, Musetti and Graham both were really good guys, and I never told them. Hell, I don't believe I ever complimented them about anything, and that's the 'damn shame.'"

"I don't guess I did either," I added ruefully.

"Me neither," David said, "and you're right. They were damn good guys."

"Yeah, you know, it just ain't right that we're sitting here now, now that they can't hear us and have no idea how we thought about them, and we're saying all these things, complimenting them and stuff, you know," Billy continued, "and they can't hear it. Don't mean nothing at all, now."

"It's a buncha shit, really," he said becoming more and more animated and agitated. "When we're alive, we never know if someone admires something about us or anything. We have to damn die to hear all that and hell, if God hasn't seen fit to allow us to eavesdrop on our funeral from above, you know, we may never know. Once we're dead, we're a wonderful this and that, but as long as we're alive, unless someone tells us different, we go around all day thinking we're nothing more than another peanut-headed, broke-dick so and so."

"Yeah, you're right, Billy," David added. David usually agreed with Billy when he was getting agitated about something. The very act of agreeing always calmed him a bit.

"Actually," David continued, holding a finger in the air as if a thought had just struck him, "come to think about it, if your friends don't say these things about you, since most folks kinda have a little lower opinion of themselves, you may just go to your grave thinking you're less than what you really are."

"Yeah, dammit," Billy continued, "it ain't right. And now Musetti and Graham are gone, and I never told them that they were great guys. I never told Musetti, for instance, that I liked talking to him cause he was a good listener, or Graham that I felt better when he was on my boat on patrols cause he never panicked when things got hairy."

"Just shoulda told them," he added, quieting now, as if tired.

"At least Jack's gonna be okay," David said.

"Yeah, I heard he was coming back to the unit as soon as the docs release him," I said. "Sure as hell will be glad to see him."

"Me too," Billy added.

"Yeah," David said. "He's gonna be strung out for a while though. He'll need us just to help him unwind from that crap."

We drank quietly for a minute, lost in our own thoughts about Jack and Graham and Musetti and about the things we'd failed to say, and probably about whether we'd say them now if we had the chance. Men have a hard time with that, and men in Vietnam seem to think it's a curse to compliment each other, almost like delivering a eulogy in expectation of an imminent need for it.

"You know, Westmoreland has all his line officers write their own eulogy before they ever go into battle," Billy said.

"Ha," David chuckled, "wouldn't you love to read some of that crap?"

"Yeah, I think it's some sort of psychological thing for them, kinda, you know," Billy continued searching for words, "like sort of taking that off the table so they'd just kinda prepare to die, so they wouldn't worry about it."

"That wasn't what I was talking about though," Billy said. It was obvious that this was important to him and just as obvious that it was something hard for him to discuss.

"I'm just saying, maybe I shoulda said something to them when they were alive, just to let them know that they were good guys, you know?"

"I don't know," I added. "If you walk around thinking like that, you gotta also walk around looking at folks and thinking, 'That guy just might be dead tomorrow.' That'd be a real drag on a person. I mean I know we stand a pretty good chance of getting popped any day, but I just don't think it's a good idea to remind ourselves of it all the time."

"Hell, Billy," David said. "You're always saying something nice about folks."

"Thanks, David," Billy smiled and slapped him gently on the back. "Nicest thing anyone ever said to me."

Musetti and Graham were the first to be killed after I arrived. Men in Vietnam had weird ways of cataloguing and compartmentalizing their time in country, and one of those was by the individuals in their unit who were killed while they were in country. Maybe it was a way of calculating our own odds of getting it. Maybe the odds were a little greater each time someone we knew was killed. We'd lose more folks throughout my first tour, and I'd learn a little more each time how to handle it and how to handle the idea of death getting a little closer. Musetti and Graham were lessons number one and two, and it bothered me that I hadn't known them better. Billy's words also bothered me, and for a long time after that I'd walk around looking at folks just thinking about what I might want to say to them. I never did that with Billy and David and Jack and the guys I was closest to though. That lesson would come later.

15

A SLIGHTLY SKEWED
SORT OF BALANCE

Americans depend on a type of balance in life. We go about our daily routines, moving from one aspect of balance to another. At the end of the day, we rest comfortably in the thought that we did our part to maintain balance; God is in His Heaven, and all is right with the world.

Of course, occasionally someone in our world gets upset with us, or the car has a flat, or the mail is late, or the newspaper doesn't arrive on time, and imbalance is temporarily introduced into our world. When this happens, we take the steps necessary to return our world to balance, and then we go on with life.

Vietnam presented a whole new challenge in terms of maintaining a balance. One of the most impacting aspects of balance, or the lack thereof, was dealing with wives, girlfriends, or significant others back home. This was complicated, of course, by the fact that there was no way to talk to them personally unless it was an extreme emergency.

Guys who came to Vietnam having left a wife or girlfriend back home were constantly deluged with stories of "Jodys" lurking in the bushes. A Jody was a term from the World War II era for some guy back home who preyed on the lonesome wife or girlfriend. The threat of a Jody was almost always on the minds of many of the younger guys. I spent a lot of time thanking the good Lord that I had no such challenge to my personal sense of balance, having nether wife nor girl waiting for me.

"You know, there's about a hundred reasons to get married," said Danny Kay, a grizzled old chief petty officer who'd married and divorced on a regular basis, and often got a kick out of adding fuel to the fire, "but there's only one right one. That means you got a 100 to 1 chance of getting it right. Course the more times you do it, the better your odds are."

Of course, in Vietnam, balance was a state of mind unknown to most.

15. A Slightly Skewed Sort of Balance

In a sense, there was no such thing as balance there. Balance in the sense we had grown used to it back home would have been imbalance in Vietnam. Things weren't supposed to equal out there, and if they did, something was wrong.

The most egregious forces of imbalance were present in every waking moment. If we were to have awoken one day and seen calm, or an absence of chaos, we'd probably have thought we'd died during the night and were drifting around in some sort of wonderland purgatory or something.

Some liked to pride themselves on thinking they had grown accustomed to the chaos and confusion, but those were usually the ones who stayed in country, intent on pushing their luck till it ran out or, if forced to leave that place, returned to a normalcy they could never live with. They had long since foregone the search for balance and replaced it with a search for the rush of near death.

"You're either going to be a cop or a crook," Jack chuckled one day as we contemplated our "post–Vietnam" existence. "Just plan on it, man. I know wherefrom I cometh. There's only two places back home that you can get the rush, and that's robbing banks or catching folks who rob banks."

"Nahh," I replied. "I don't buy it."

Of course, Jack was right again. He may not have known it at the time; he probably heard some other folks talk about it, but he was right. Statistics proved in the years immediately following Vietnam, fighting crime and committing crime were two highly likely vocations for Vietnam vets.

We spent a lot of time talking about such inane things. It was our way of seeking balance at times when we didn't even realize we had lost it. Still in the "pre–Tet" phase of the war, we were intent on doing our patrols, counting the days (we counted backwards in those days, beginning with 364 and a wake-up), and talking about the things we did before and the things we intended to do afterward.

We'd sit on the edge of our bunks after a patrol, whether it was 0600 or 1800, passing a quart of Jack Daniels back and forth. We would take a healthy swig and chase the burn with drags on a cigarette while we told each other stories about life and family back home.

"I ain't kiddin' ya, man, my sister/cousin/neighbor is the prettiest girl in the whole county. I can fix ya up with her if you want me to," we'd say. "Besides when we get back home, you gotta come go fishing/hunting/hiking with me."

It was our way of assuring ourselves that there was something after this.

Brothers in the Mekong Delta

There would be a home where balance was an easy fix, and no one would be shooting at us. The things we saw every day were things we were supposed to see, things that gave proof that the world was in balance and God was *actually* in Heaven and all was *actually* right with the world. Of course, in those days, we were convinced that was what would make us happy, that "back home" simple: balance and calm.

We'd tell stories of home, stories with such detail and descriptive verbiage as to recreate entire communities and settings where happy times flowed like rivers. In all honesty, we were talking to ourselves more than to each other. Recreating home was a way of assuring ourselves of something we might lose if we didn't keep sealing it in our subconscious. We just wanted to make sure we didn't forget, that the normalcy we had known wasn't replaced in our mind with that which existed in our current world.

"My dad," Jack said, one early morning as we sat and drank and smoked, "knows every fishing spot in McClain County, Oklahoma. Every Easter, we go looking for mushrooms, and my mom cooks them in egg batter. Damn, they're good, Godfrey. You gotta come there when we all get back."

We'd just returned from a night patrol. As we sat on bunks across from each other, Jack pulled our bottle of JD from his locker. He lit a cigarette and took the first swig, grimaced from the burn and passed it to me. A good deep drag on the cigarette took some of the sting out of it.

"Hell, yeah," I added eloquently, trying to suppress a cough, as the beginnings of a buzz lightened my head. "I can't wait."

You could almost tell how long a person had been in country from the subject of his conversations. The normalcy we tried to keep alive at first—the normal of home—gradually gave way to the normal of Vietnam. It's hard to tell when it happens, but one day you just shift your focus.

"You think I'm kidding," I choked out one evening, wagging my finger instructively, as I waited for the burn from a deep pull on the bottle to cease and my voice to fully return. "We picked him up, and his damn arm just fell completely off, like there was nothing attaching it to his shoulder at all. It just fell the hell completely off onto the ground. Damnedest thing I ever saw."

There were two absolute requirements in dealing emotionally with the incongruities of Vietnam, incongruities such as an arm falling off a seemingly intact, albeit dead, human body. You had to make some sort of sick joke or attempt at humor, and you had to dehumanize your enemy (and in many cases your allies), especially when they were dead.

"Yeah, we got a call to go help evacuate some ARVNs from up at that outpost that got hit this week," I continued before pausing for a second to take another swig from the bottle. "They got their asses kicked in that fight."

"Yeah," Billy chimed in while I was gasping. "Hell, they put the worst folks they have out there to defend those little outposts anyhow. Doesn't take a lot for Charlie to wipe-em out."

I was anxious for the conversation to stay centered on what I had seen and experienced and not get sidetracked on to the capability of ARVN (Army of the Republic of Vietnam) soldiers. As soon as I got my voice back I continued, "Yeah, and man, we could smell it before we got ½ klick out. Hell, we didn't know they wanted us to bring the bodies back too. Those guys had been dead since the day before, just laying out there in the sun."

A lot of things had changed after Musetti and Graham had been killed, and Jack had been wounded. Guys had been shifted around to different boats. The bosses were like a bunch of women just moving into a new apartment and not knowing where to put the furniture, constantly shifting everything around. I had been assigned to another boat the day before, and Jack was being held back from patrols until they figured he was ready to hit it again.

"It was funny," I continued reflectively, "but once we tied off and got into the area, the damn smell just sort of went away; I mean I know it was still there, but I just didn't notice it as much. Funny."

David always felt he had a responsibility to try and explain the unexplainable. "Yeah, it doesn't really look like that; it's just the way the light reflects off it," or "The damn AKs sound that way at night because of the temperature change, you know," were typical of his efforts.

"The smell was still there," he suggested. "It was just overwhelmed by the sight of the bodies when you got closer. Your sense of sight took all the juice out of your sense of smell."

"Ain't that right? Uh-huh?" David said as he jabbed Billy good-naturedly.

"Uh-huh," Billy dutifully replied, drawing out the "huhhhh" response, mimicking the voice of a child.

There was an old *Little Rascals* segment in which one of the characters was nicknamed "Uh-huh" because he never said anything but "Uh-huh." "Uh-huh" was always sought out by the others for affirmation, assured of finding it when they asked, "Ain't that right, Uh-huh?" David and Billy relied on the digression when a conversation got involved or emotional or heated, or when David wasn't really sure his "explanation" was correct and needed the endorsement. It always worked.

"Yeah, I guess," I replied while Jack and Billy nodded in agreement, "but it was still weird. Me and Ron Lake picked this one guy up to put him in a body bag. I grabbed him by the shirt at his shoulders and Ron grabbed his legs, and man, when we picked him up, his arm just slipped out of his shirt sleeve and fell on the ground."

"Shit," Jack grimaced. "Course I guess he really didn't need it anymore."

David spit whiskey on the floor, choking out a horselaugh. Billy just shook his head and smiled signifying his approval, and in spite of myself, I too chuckled. It really wasn't that funny, but that was the way we handled things.

We had earned the right to be crass and even to say things that were dehumanizing at times. None of us meant it or even really felt it. I was always impressed with the way Billy and Jack and David interacted with the locals and with the interpreters who patrolled with us. Billy, always willing to throw a punch or two just to change the subject, would often offer to defend our interpreter when anyone criticized or demeaned him.

It was necessary to laugh at the dead you didn't know. It was necessary to use terms like "slope" or "gook." It was necessary to criticize the seemingly idle manner of the locals when they suffered a casualty in the family. But, when we were alone and had no one to talk to but ourselves and God, we made amends, to ourselves and to God, sort of like confession.

Of course, the confessions you make to your brothers don't really mean anything. When you confess to a brother, you know you're free from judgments, kind of like one alcoholic telling another alcoholic all the bad things they've done when drunk. It's the things you tell the outside world, out loud, that count. Those are the words that absolve you. At the time, asking God for forgiveness was just necessary. It was just another way we sought a balance that, in that place, in that time, just didn't exist.

16

An Everlasting Thanksgiving Memory

Section 513 was blessed to have the best cook in the entire United States military. Eddy Flurry, a grizzled old chief petty officer, was not only a good cook; he relished the process. It was almost as though every meal he cooked was intended as a last meal for his mother or father.

The cook tent itself was set up to resemble, as much as possible, your grandmother's kitchen back home. The stove was old, black iron with a chimney piped out through the top of the tent. Flurry cooked in large pots, leaving them simmering on the stove for everyone to serve themselves, just like one might at home. Yet he was an artist at using local produce and spices.

Flurry got most of the supplies and ingredients he used from the States. The one thing he couldn't have shipped from home was the flour for bread, so he purchased that on the local market. Every day with this flour, he baked loaves of bread that were so aromatic, the smell of them baking seemed to drift all the way to the boat pier.

The bread did have one little drawback, though some saw it as a plus; the flour came, at no extra charge, infused with flour weevils too small to extract, but just large enough to allow one to distinguish them from, say … pepper, due to the tiny little weevil legs protruding out of the tiny little weevil bodies.

"It's okay," Billy chuckled one day when I first noticed them. "If you're in a hurry, just grab a slab of bread, and you get your protein mixed in for you."

A few days after the Tet offensive, when we were still operating at an upgraded tempo but things seemed to be scaling down a bit, the cook announced he was going to prepare a winter feast similar to Thanksgiving, complete with a huge turkey using his family's secret method. He promised us all that once we'd tasted it, it would become the basis from which we would measure all future Thanksgiving or Christmas turkeys. As we knew his reputation and skill, we also knew this was no idle promise.

In the days leading up to the special meal, anticipation built at a steady pace. The stress of post–Tet operations lessened a bit, and it seemed we could almost smell roasting turkey, though the big meal was still a week away.

Jack and I drew night patrol, beginning at midnight, the day of the big meal. All night long, we alternated between moments of apprehension, the new apprehension we had come to know since Tet, and idle chatter about the big meal that day. Such was the reputation of our cook that our saliva-producing, Pavlovian instincts kicked in regularly throughout the night.

Obviously, no one on the boat drew a C-rations meal that evening before the patrol, and long before we headed in, our stomachs began to growl. The anticipation was such that we even suggested ways to consume as much turkey as possible.

"Look, man," Jack offered, "it's easy. All you got to do is eat as much as you can, then get up and walk around the compound fence a couple of times. By the time you get back to the chow tent, your stomach will stretch, and you can damn near eat another full meal."

We secured the boat after patrol that morning around 0600 and went back to our tent. Though we fancied we could smell turkey and dressing cooking already, it was still hours away from the big meal. We decided to partake in our usual ritual of sitting on the edge of our cots, smoking cigarettes and swapping a bottle of Jack Daniels back and forth, while we verbally dissected the night's patrol. The conversation this morning, however, was different. We talked of the coming meal and of all the past Christmases and Thanksgivings we'd shared with family back home. Having exhausted the pertinent issues, and half the quart of Jack Daniels, we simply kicked back on the cots and passed out.

The next thing I remember is Jack grabbing me by my big toe, shaking and screaming, "Get up, Godfrey! Get the hell up and get dressed. It's one o'clock, and we're missing dinner. Man, get the hell out of bed."

My head splitting and still dizzy from the drinking, I jumped into my pants, pulled my boots on but left them untied, and grabbed a shirt as we dashed out of the tent opening and stumbled toward the cook tent.

Our compound was small enough that virtually every tent and structure was visible from just about any point. The cook tent was situated in the center of the camp. As we rushed toward the steps leading up to the front door, we could see through the open tent flaps that the Vietnamese cook assistants were sweeping and mopping the floor. The usual, small line of folks waiting to get in wasn't there.

Our cook had an old hound dog that he'd rescued sometime before I arrived. The dog had quickly become a camp mascot and been affectionately dubbed Red Dog for obvious reasons. As we approached the steps to the tent, we were aghast at the sight of Red Dog, lounging on the bottom step, contentedly gnawing on the remains of a huge turkey carcass.

We stopped in our tracks, mouths open, and dropped to the steps, halfway between moaning from hangovers and succumbing to tears of disappointment. As we sat there in our dismal state, our heads banging, the cook stepped through the door.

"What the hell is wrong with you two?" he asked.

I looked at Red Dog, then up at him, the glare of the bright sun causing me to wince. "We got drunk and missed your turkey dinner, dammit."

Jack just nodded his head, saying nothing.

The cook laughed out loud for what seemed a full minute. The anger and outrage at his taunting seemed to exacerbate the pain in my head.

Just as I was about to protest, he said, "I can't believe this. You fools! Hell, you were in here four hours ago. You both ate three damn plates of food. Don't you remember?"

He turned and walked back into the cook tent, still laughing uncontrollably. I looked at Jack in dismay and confusion.

"You know," he said, "come to think of it, I ain't a bit hungry."

17

TET: END OF THE SIMPLE PUSH-PULL

B y Christmas 1967, I had been in country for seven months. I had long since settled into the routine, and though I was still learning, had been assigned my own boat crew. The promotion was in a normal line of progression, since most folks got their own crew with that amount of time, though I secretly chose to believe it was because of some leadership qualities I possessed.

Folks grew up fast in Vietnam, but at only 20 years old, I would be a decade or so in understanding what it meant to be a true leader. The pre–Tet job, however, was still routine enough that almost anyone could do it. We patrolled a specific area with inlets and canals we had grown to know like the veins in our arms, stopped boats we saw as potential trouble, and responded to support calls from other units when we needed to. Everybody knew their jobs and knew everyone else's job too. When the rockets hit or the snap of automatic weapons pierced the quiet, no one needed to be told what to do.

I did know enough about leadership, however, to know that I couldn't ask anyone to do something I wasn't willing to do myself. I knew that our daily routine had the potential to be stressful and dangerous, and that it was necessary to add as much levity as possible. My guys, like those on many boat crews, didn't wear uniforms, per se. Cutoff camos, t-shirts, and deck sandals were standard for those who chose them. Of course, flak jackets and helmets were close at hand, but unless we were going into one of the canals or tributaries we knew to be "hot areas," we didn't wear them.

The risk we all knew and all lived with was that if we were engaged by rocket attack or automatic weapons in an area where we hadn't expected it, and were therefore not wearing jackets and helmets, we would have no time to grab them before we had to take evasive action and fight back.

17. Tet

Vietnam wasn't a clean war. Years later, following a lengthy break in service, I reentered the U.S. Army Special Forces and fought in Afghanistan. Though Afghanistan too, was chaotic, military engagements, missions, and operations were normally undertaken following a period of time of preparation.

Missions in Afghanistan were planned and often rehearsed for at least a week. Soldiers in Afghanistan were almost always prepped and equipped for any possible contingency before a patrol. Combat operations in Afghanistan, either planned or impromptu, were always followed, rightly so, by lengthy AARs (After Action Reviews).

Missions in Vietnam were conceived in the morning and carried out in the evening. In Vietnam we were occasionally fired upon and entered into a pretty hairy firefight in the morning, returned to base to re-equip, and went back on patrol, occasionally re-engaging the same enemy force before sundown.

Though we were all trained pretty well before deploying to Vietnam, once in country, we realized that there were no training protocols that could

Aftermath of relatively minor firefight. One wounded crew member was laid on the deck during retreat, while he was being treated.

have equipped us for what we encountered. It wasn't a "textbook" counter-insurgency and became more and more unconventional on a daily basis.

In hindsight, that wasn't necessarily a bad thing. From an operational standpoint, the fewer rules and protocols there were, the fewer rules you'd break, and the fewer protocols you'd violate. The special operations guys would often hash out a pretty hairy mission over beers, and execute, as soon as possible, after sobering up. PBR crews were given a proportionate amount of freedom, and though it has never been calculated, we probably met with much of our success precisely because we operated like that.

Still, under the circumstances, the pre–Tet war in Vietnam did seem to be somewhat of a chess game, with neither side gaining a great deal or losing a great deal. Something was brewing in those days, however; something was different. Though few of us talked about it, or even realized it completely, there was definitely something in the air in the months leading up to the end of 1967, and we all felt it.

"You now that funny feeling you get when a storm is brewing?" Jack mused one day, as we broke out the Jack Daniels and began our usual routine.

Instead of slouching on our bunks, this time we were in the weapons shed, a workshop of sorts for minor weapons repair and maintenance. Jack had been pulled off patrol and assigned there, wounded yet again, only this time by a rat; no doubt a Vietcong rat, but a rat nonetheless.

Reaching under a box of fifty caliber ammo to load it onto a boat during patrol prep one day, he was bitten by the saboteur. Rehab for him this time involved being pulled from patrol duties and assigned to the weapons shed. He also had to receive weekly injections in the stomach with a needle that seemed about a foot long and as thick as a pencil.

Usually we spent an hour or so in the evening drinking whiskey, smoking cigarettes, and taking turns reading *No Time for Sergeants* out loud. We laughed like school kids at the main character, Will Stockdale. Lately, however, a somewhat ominous change in the air left us in no mood for Will Stockdale.

"Yeah," I replied. "Actually, I been sort of feeling something weird lately, and I know some of the other guys have too."

"I just kinda feel like something's gonna happen soon, but I don't know what, you know," he added.

I took another swig, coughed, and lit a new cigarette from the still hot glow of the one I had smoked down to the filter.

"David said something like that yesterday. He said he thought people were kinda looking at us different and changing routines and stuff," I offered. "Course it could just be that we all hang around each so much that we've become a risk to each other. You know like two people who've been married too long and start to think alike, and shit like that."

We didn't know it at the time, of course, but things were changing and toward a specific end. The VC had been moving men and equipment into strategic areas for weeks. Most American units around the country were being engaged in small skirmishes, test attacks, sort of like practice basketball games before the big tournament. These test attacks usually involved short contacts followed by hasty retreats into the jungle. They were occurring with more and more frequency. A storm was brewing, and you could tell it, just as you could feel a drop in temperature shortly before the thunder and smell the clean air just as the wind begins to whip up.

One of the tragedies of Vietnam was that someone, somewhere, always knew these things, and in keeping with the old adage that "Knowledge is power," they didn't often pass it along. Intelligence acquired and collated in Saigon was rarely shared to the extent it should have been, and even if it had been, we would have been the last to receive it. We were still the "flea on the donkey's ass," and our world consisted of nothing past that which we could see. It was enough though. We were used to relying on our own instincts and not expecting a lot of data from the intel end. Our gut kicked in, and we sensed something different. Unable to put a finger on it though, the "pre–Tet" push-pull operational tempo was still the rule of the day, right up until late on the night of January 29, 1968.

18

DRUMS AND BUGLES

January 29, 1968, fell on a Monday. For Vietnam vets, that particular night was one that would never be forgotten, and little things, ordinarily inconsequential things about it stuck with us forever, just as many can recall what they were doing when John Kennedy was killed.

My boat was part of a patrol assigned to night shift, which meant we were to be on the river and fully operational by 2300 hours. That evening, we loaded our boats as usual, checking all necessities, and pulled out of the harbor, coasting gently out the canal toward the entrance to the river.

Looking back, I can still remember everything. Even the dimly lit, waning moon, casting a beautiful glow across the water as we moved out through the canal, remains vivid in my mind. Sadec was virtually empty but, with a standing curfew in place, such was normal for that time of night. It didn't register at the time, but in the aftermath, it made perfect sense. The far horizon, normally dotted here and there in the distance with sporadic light from firefights, was as quiet and as dark as if it were a huge cornfield in Nebraska. It was almost eerie.

The moon was fading but had not yet gone completely dark. It was during this lunar phase that our starlight scopes began to lose effectiveness. While the starlight scope allowed some limited visibility at night, human movement, seen as greenish figures, could be spotted through the scopes only if there were some natural moonlight. During the waning and new moon phase, the scopes were of little use.

The night was unusually comfortable with the humidity barely noticeable. We slipped out into the middle of the river where both boats cut engines and drifted south toward Vinh Long, a sizeable city with another PBR section 35 klicks away. As we drifted quietly, we checked visibility through the starlight scopes and cleaned the river vines that often got sucked into the interior screw-type shafts under the engine covers. We checked our C-ration boxes, swapping some items among ourselves, discarding the ones no one wanted over the side, and talked quietly. There was no reason to maintain silence that far out into the river. Smoking cigarettes, however, was always an art form. The glow from the tip could be seen for miles, so when you took a drag, you cupped your hands. It didn't really work that well, but gave us some sense of minimal security. Charlie always knew where we were though. The senses—sight as well as smell and hearing—were automatically heightened at night.

Normally, when drifting with the engines silent, we could kick back and listen to the sounds of sporadic firefights as far as 50 kilometers away: the staccato "tat-tat-tat" of AK-47s, the slower, thudding, rapid fire of 50-caliber machine guns, and an occasional mortar round or B40 rocket.

Usually the night sounds were like the crickets or frogs back home, and we paid no more attention than we would to the sounds from our childhood. If we noticed, no one mentioned it, but that night there was nothing. The night brought one of those quiets that prompted you to whisper, even though there was no reason to do so.

We had drifted 10 or 12 klicks south and were gearing up to fire the engines and head back north to our patrol sector. Suddenly, just as I was about to start the engines, the whole world to the south of us lit up. The sight was reminiscent of old, Cold War era, educational videos we were made to watch in high school back in the early '60s. In them, a bomb would go off on a distant horizon in the middle of the night, turning darkness to a mixture of gold and white, promising worldwide destruction.

Seconds later, the sounds reached us, multiple explosions combined with relentless automatic weapons fire with no lull in intensity. Vinh Long was in serious trouble.

"Son of a bitch," was all we could say, and we all said it multiple times in a matter of seconds as we scrambled to prep for one hell of a fight.

"See that?" Chief Kay on the lead boat shouted into the radio from our command boat a few yards away, though there was little I could have done to avoid seeing it. "We gotta head their way. Call command and tell them Vinh Long's under attack, and we're going south to assist."

I keyed the mike on the radio as I swung the boat around behind the command boat, by this time on a full-speed track heading south. "Cougat, Cougat, Cougat Charlie," I barked into the mike. "Vinh Long is under serious attack. Request permission to proceed south to assist."

"Negative, negative!" The unusually excited response from our command in Sadec was spontaneous and urgent. "RTB (return to base) immediately.

We're receiving incoming mortar and automatic weapons fire as well. Repeat, we are also under attack. RTB ASAP."

Our lead boat made a sharp U-turn as we followed close behind. Heading back north, I glanced over my shoulder and saw the intense, sporadic brightness from exploding ordinance continuing around Vinh Long. My crew was prepping for a serious fight, their movements automatic and reflexive. There was no mistaking the anxious looks on their faces, however, as they glanced at each other inquisitively.

The American presence and the 513 and PBR operations in Vinh Long were situated mostly on the outskirts of the city. As a result, launching an attack there wasn't extremely difficult to coordinate. Hitting larger riverine bases like Vinh Long was routine, a continuation of the pre–Tet, push-pull process. They'd been targeted before, although never with this intensity.

An attack on Sadec, on the other hand, had to involve a significant "balls out" effort on the part of the enemy. Sadec was an inland community, and our base was located in the center of the town. It was possible that some who lived there were sympathetic to the VC or NVA, but the vast majority of Sadec was firmly supportive of our presence and opposed to the Communist insurgency. An attack there had to be extremely determined since the attackers would have to either infiltrate from the perimeter or actually fight their way in, coming close enough to make automatic weapons and small arms effective.

The bottom line, and we all knew it, was that what we were seeing represented a definite risk by the enemy. If they were unsuccessful, they'd experience a severe setback. We knew they wouldn't undertake such a venture unless they knew what they were doing and were totally committed to winning. What we didn't know, at the time, was that we were witnessing firsthand, up close and very personal, the 1968 Tet Offensive. From our little vantage point, the ass end of the donkey, we were witnessing only a very small part of it. The era of push-pull was definitely over, and in that moment, everyone knew it.

Sadec was 30 minutes away. We hung close to the western side of the river since our entrance into Sadec involved a sharp westward turn when we reached the canal, and we didn't want to waste time. Normally, especially at night, we'd remain as far out in the river's heart as possible to discourage attack from the shore, but there was absolutely nothing normal about this night.

Situated sporadically along the western bank of the Mekong River were several smaller South Vietnamese army outposts. These outposts were usually occupied by a dozen soldiers, many with families, posted there as security for the area. The soldiers that occupied these postings were often the youngest and least experienced.

As a part of the overall Tet attack, the NVA had launched smaller attacks on virtually every one of these outposts. The chaos and panic that ensued resulted in wild, defensive fire from these posts in every direction, including ours. As we sped north, we received sporadic automatic weapons fire from every outpost we passed.

From the coxswain position, driving the boat, I had little visual capability. The bow of the boat at high speed was six feet out of the water, and a small ¼-inch armor plate to my left rose up to shoulder level. I could still see, however, over the top of the plate.

The unmistakable tracer signature of automatic weapons fire in our direction gave me an indication of how accurate the panicked fire was. To this day, I remember watching the bright red of the tracers coming in my direction until they faded, then briefly ducking behind the armor plate to safety. I repeated the process dozens of times that night, each time we passed one of the small forts, speeding toward Sadec. In actuality, the effort would have been futile if a round had been accurate enough to reach me, but it gave me an unfounded, fleeting sense of security.

The surreal nature of that night was compounded by the sounds. We were accustomed to the sounds of firefights, the tat-tat of automatic fire, the telltale thump of launched mortars followed by explosions, and the sharp whacking sound of launched rockets. These were expected sounds, and as such drew little of our attention, blending into the whole like the moan of the cello or the tinkling of a triangle in an orchestra.

Other sounds we heard that night, however, just didn't belong, and though they were not as loud, they stood out as sharply as if they had been launched through the loudest of PA systems. All through the night, mixed in with the expected sounds of battle, were the unmistakable tones of bugles and the pounding notes of deep, bellowing drums.

The bugles were distinctive. They could have been reproduced from an old John Wayne cavalry movie signaling the imminent arrival of rescue. Only here there was no discernable pattern, just shrill wails, loud enough to be heard and distinguished above the traditional sounds of war. The drums too, were easily heard over the din, and were reminiscent of communications between native tribes in old Tarzan movies I'd seen as a kid. Each time we heard them on the trip back up the river, we couldn't help shooting each other that familiar "WTF (what the fuck) is that?" glance. The WTF glance was always uncomfortable for us. It signaled the presence of something we had no idea how to deal with. In hindsight, that entire night and the following weeks elicited a plethora of WTF glances.

In the weeks that followed, we learned that since radio communications for the VC and NVA were unreliable, they had developed a sophisticated system of bugle and drum communications.

Tet ushered in an era of confusion and chaos for months to come. Though some intelligence factions in Saigon had had the same "Something wicked this way comes" feelings we'd had for a while, they couldn't explain them any more than we could. The short of it was that people expected something, but no one expected the Tet offensive. As such, little had been done to prepare for it.

Such unpreparedness and lack of foresight was not unusual for politicians, since they rarely had a clue anyhow, but for those a little lower down the ladder, the planners and the purveyors of strategy, it was devastating. Ironically, being caught by surprise and being ill-prepared for such an all-out offensive was fortuitous for some.

For those who wanted to make a name for themselves, it was a zenith of sorts. Virtually anyone with an idea was heard, and many of those ideas which, in the pre–Tet phase of the war, would not even have been considered were now fast-tracked.

For the lovers of war, for the lovers of adventure, Vietnam was now Sutter's Mill. Anything anyone did in those days following Tet was considered "the right thing to do at the time." Tet and the aftermath represented a whole new vein of gold being discovered. For us, however, for the guys riding the PBRs, for the guys in 513, the order of the day was "Tie a knot in the rope where you are at that moment and hold on tight."

Little did we know, that night signaled the end of any perceived, pre–Tet phase of operations. The "Vietnam experience," however that was defined, for every single person in the country changed that night—better for some, worse for others—but for all, it changed.

19

POST TET:
A NEW BALLGAME

Neither Vinh Long nor Sadec had been primary targets of the NVA and VC that night. In true guerrilla fashion, these locations were hit, engaged long enough to elicit a formidable response, then abandoned by the insurgents.

We arrived back at base and were folded into the base defense protocol immediately. The full attack involved a few rockets, mortars, and short barrages of automatic weapons fire. Nothing was hit and no one was injured. However, since we had never before experienced an attack of that magnitude so close in to the interior of Sadec, we all had the crap scared out of us for a bit.

Major cities such as Saigon in the south and Hue in the north saw extensive fighting. The enemy was seriously intent on taking Hue down and seizing permanent control of several key locations in and around Saigon.

In the months that followed Tet, however, and precisely because of it, everything changed for us. The American military has almost always been successful in battles and wars because we think ahead and plan ahead. The war in Vietnam was run by politicians rather than soldier commanders. As such, we never planned ahead. We reacted.

Our patrol rotations and functions were seriously altered, and normalcy, in the sense that we knew it, never returned. Immediately following the initial Tet offensive, because the fighting was still fierce in many larger cities, our patrols were sent to various locations where we could be effective; our mission was fire support for the units engaged there.

The following day, five PBR crews were sent to Chau Doc city, 20 klicks south of Sadec, to carry out firing runs through the canal-like waterways in the city where the VC were holed up in the buildings.

"Man, I felt like we were in Venice, Italy, shooting up a bunch of Italian villas along the canals," David said a few days after their return. "We'd load up, make a run at high speed through the canals, whipping in and out of the turns, all the while shooting at anything that moved in the buildings that lined the waterways. Then we'd clear the area out on the other side of the city, load up again, and make another run. Damnedest thing I ever saw."

A virtual Wild West-type firefight continued in Chau Doc for days, with the boats flying full speed through the city, firing with their fifties at the buildings that lined the canals, then regrouping and returning for another run. Other boats went ashore and secured landing areas for medevac choppers, conducted resupply runs for units in the city, and evacuated some civilian and military casualties.

Two additional patrols were sent to An Phu Special Forces camp to help defend the base and resupply the defenders. Two additional boats were also sent to Cao Lanh Ferry landing which had been overrun by a force of 200 VC. Following a serious two-day firefight there, local forces backed by our patrols regained control of the landing.

Missions such as these continued at the same operational tempo for several weeks. We eventually took up our standard mission of policing the river for contraband and infiltration, but the main mission of PBRs in the entire country became one of assisting other units, mostly SEAL teams in offensive operations, and fighting our way out of surprise attacks. In pre–Tet we were conducting patrols on a rotation of three days on, one day off. Post-Tet saw us in a consistent 12 on, 12 off status that remained in effect.

In the immediate aftermath of the initial attacks, we maintained a mission status for six days with no down time. It was during this period that I was introduced to the miracle drug, Dexedrine.

The night we returned to defend Sadec, arriving back at base and taking up positions about one in the morning, began the longest period of time I'd ever gone with no sleep. Years later, I reentered the military following a long break in service, this time in Army Special Forces, and became accustomed to training and mission regimes in which sleep was virtually non-existent. In Vietnam I was still a kid, as were we all. None of us had outgrown that ability to sleep long hours.

The enemy attack on Sadec had pretty much ended by the time we arrived back at base that first night, but we had no way of knowing that. I had taken up a position along the base perimeter with Jack, Billy, and David, and for more than three hours, we peered across the sites of our M16s into the night, absolutely certain we would be reduced to hand to hand combat, repelling hordes of invaders at any moment. As it happened, the only thing we lost was several hours of rest, and though I didn't know it at the time, such would be the case for many days to come.

The first rays of light from the new day peered over the horizon to our backs around 0530. As is always the case, some level of optimism returned with our ability to actually see what was in front of us. Our base was surrounded by civilization, and in spite of the attack the night before, everything seemed to be in its place. No "scorched earth" was apparent, though few civilians had ventured out, leaving the area with a ghostly feel.

We looked at each other, not really knowing what to say. Following a few obligatory "son of a bitches" and "motherfuckers," assuring all of us a mutual feeling of "knowing nothing better to say," we breathed a sigh of relief. It was then that I realized how sore and depleted I was.

"Damn man," I muttered. "I am sore as hell. Feel like I've run ten miles to get here."

"Yeah, me too," Jack said. "We've been keyed up all night, waiting to get our asses shot off. Hell of a night, huh."

"Man, you should have been with us last night." I began reconstructing events. "We were down by Vinh Long, and they got their asses lit up. I mean all hell broke loose."

"We called in to get permission to assist, and that's when they told us y'all were being hit too," I continued, my shoulders aching each time I raised my arm for emphasis. "What the hell do you suppose all that was about? I mean it sure as hell wasn't a coincidence and get this; all the way back up the river, the damn ARVNS from the outposts were shooting at us. Damnedest thing I ever saw; I mean why the hell were they shooting at us?"

"Hell, those guys probably didn't know who they were shooting at. Musta been as scared as the rest of us," David added.

"Maybe," I said, "but I don't understand why they figured Charlie was going to be on the river. And get this, the weirdest thing, all the way back I kept hearing these damn drums and bugles. Swear to God, man, sounded like a movie combination of *She Wore a Yellow Ribbon* and *Tarzan, the Ape Man*."

Just then, we got the "All clear" and "Secure from post" calls. We stood slowly, stretching the kinks out of our arms and legs.

"Wonder if 'Cookie' has been able to get anything ready to eat. I'm starved," Jack said.

Brothers in the Mekong Delta

As we moved slowly toward the makeshift mess hall tent, still glancing out at the town, we could hear distant fighting at a level more intense than usual. Just then Ed Strazalkowski from the command shed came around the corner.

Ski, as we called him, was from New Jersey and had a noticeable accent. He was a twitchy, nervous guy under normal circumstances and seemed to take pride in the fact that Jack thought he was a member of the Mafia back home. As he rounded the corner and walked deliberately toward us that morning, however, he seemed much more nervous than usual.

"Grab a bite, Godfrey, and do it in a hurry. You too, Billy and David," he added. "You guys are going out in one hour."

"Going out where?" Billy asked.

"People are getting shot up all over the place, and we're getting taskings faster than we can keep up with them. Better grab an extra share of everything too," he added. "You're likely to be out for several days."

A funny thing happens when you're in the military in a combat environment, and you get urgent orders to respond to something out of the ordinary. All your bodily functions key up in biological preparation for an unknown. You suddenly feel stronger, energetic, and capable of anything. The feeling doesn't last long, but for a moment, we forgot we'd been up all night on alert.

Ski didn't slow down to answer questions. He continued his frantic pace toward others in the compound. There was little doubt that we weren't the only ones who were going to be given that same message.

"I'm gonna skip breakfast," I said as I turned toward our tent. "I need a shower and clean clothes a whole lot more, and I don't think we're going to have time for everything."

"We'll grab you a sandwich or something," Jack said, as the three of them picked up the pace toward the chow tent.

I sat on the edge of my bunk, packing a few things in a "go-bag," a small shoulder-strapped bag that was designed to heft all the things you needed to survive, if only for a few days. Normally these were kept ready to grab and run, but I had a few minutes and wanted to make sure everything I thought I'd need for an extensive patrol was there.

As I leaned back for a moment, I had an overwhelming urge to just close my eyes for a few minutes. I knew that if I did that, however, I would fall into a heavy sleep. Since I would have had only a few minutes of rest, I would be rousted up and feel twice as bad as I had before dozing off. I stood up instead, and began rotating my torso to get some flexibility into my lower back and shake off the dullness.

"Hey man, take one of these," Billy drawled as he stepped through the door of the tent and handed me a capsule. "It's Dexedrine. It'll help you stay awake. Ski gave me and David some of them. Command has ordered them issued to everyone. Know what that means, I guess."

I popped one in my mouth and threw my head back, feeling the pill slip down my throat.

"Damn good thing he did," I said. "I am tired as hell."

Outside the tent, we threw our gear on the back of the pickup and jumped in after it. The sun was in full stride by then, promising a scorcher.

"I got Ski to put all of us on the same boat. Billy'll be running the show for us, but I have a feeling we're not going to be hooked up with a standard patrol," David said.

"Matter of fact," he added, "I have a feeling nothing is going to be standard for a while."

A few minutes later, we were completing the prep on our boat and had fired the engine up. Still tied to the pier as we idled, I felt more tired and sleepy then than I had back at the tent, the sense of urgency having passed, even if only for a short while. We'd been told to get ready for something big, but as was usually the case, no one knew what the "something big" was, or where and when we would run into it.

"Are you sure those things work? The pills, I mean," I asked Billy. "Hell man. I'm still dog-tired and sleepy."

"I have no idea. Never took one before," he said.

"Well, just in case, maybe you better give me another one."

Billy handed me a small bottle containing four more tablets. I opened it and popped another in my mouth. Before pill number one had a chance to start working that morning, I took one more, making a total of three 10 milligram Dexedrine capsules floating around somewhere in my stomach.

I wasn't used to taking drugs of any kind at that time. I suppose I expected to be Superman, stepping out of a phone booth as soon as the first one had cleared my tonsils. When that didn't happen, I naturally assumed I had gotten some bad pills.

To my surprise, however, by the time we hit the main river ten minutes later, pill number one kicked in. At first, I felt exhilarated. I went from "running on fumes" to "exceeding the speed limit" immediately. I was counting the ammo in the fifties and cleaning everyone's weapons at the same time.

Brothers in the Mekong Delta

Like a first time drunk, I cut a pretty laughable figure, trying to carry on several conversations at once. All told, it was a comical diversion for us. For the moment, the confusion and chaos from the Tet attacks were replaced by the antics of a stoked-up, quirky guy from Mississippi. My first experience with speed kept me awake for the next two days and became one of the millions of times God watched over me in that I hadn't overdosed.

20

ANATOMY
OF A FIREFIGHT

For several weeks, throughout the south, units of all kinds were mired in desperate firefights. Most of the larger army infantry and marine installations fought continuous defensive skirmishes, some repelling actual hordes of NVA forces fully intent on complete victory.

Smaller ARVN units suffered the most, as vital assistance and supplies were diverted to the more important units and installations. The VC and NVA would eventually realize they weren't going to end the war, cut their losses, and retreat, but we didn't know at the time when that would happen.

When we weren't being ordered specifically to support units under attack, we simply took it upon ourselves to RTB, rearm, and go where we thought we'd be most useful. For every fighting man on both sides of the war, the intensity of Tet would be with us forever. In some areas, it seemed the ferocity of combat would never stop. In others, even though the intensity subsided a bit, we knew the war had taken on a whole new tempo—operations tempo—and it would remain with us.

Our first serious conflict that particular day, the first day following Tet, came just after nightfall. We were assigned to support an ARVN unit a few klicks north of us in an area we had affectionately dubbed "Stay-away Straits" for obvious reasons. An ARVN outpost had been hit an hour or so before the sun set as they were in the process of resupplying and refortifying. Located inside the entrance to the straits, they were engaged by more than 100 NVA, their enemy counterparts from the north. They were in grave danger of being overrun.

We reached the entrance as the dark of night completely engulfed the jungle. Firefights in Vietnam were confusing in the light of day since there were never any clear lines separating the good guys from the bad guys and seldom any visuals of your enemy. Insurgents fired at you from thickets and moved expertly from one area to the other. Rather than shooting at "someone," you were always shooting at "a vicinity," and as the target was a group of bushes or a thicket on the edge of a clearing, it never fell over, mortally wounded. Assessing progress was difficult at best. The routine was simply to keep firing in hopes your enemy would be overwhelmed and retreat.

The dark, however, added a whole new dimension of confusion. The only thing we had during those fights to guide us were tracer rounds. Tracers were loaded, generally every fourth round, specifically for this purpose. If you were fortunate enough to have a general location of your enemy, the return fire process was to walk your rounds in from the sides or from above until you were centered on your suspected target, then unload. Everyone had a preference, but I always felt more in control when I dropped fire down from above until I had centered on target. Some preferred to walk in from either side, but this worked best for me.

My method was more easily done with the 50s and the M-60s. The M16s we had access to during those years—the early models—had a serious issue with recoil movement. We were trained to fire in bursts, and most used four to six-round actions. Automatic weapons are designed for heavy concentrations of fire. Using them as single shot weapons was generally a waste of effort.

On full auto, however, even with short four-round bursts, the M16 had a tendency to rise up. If we were reduced to using them in a firefight, we often tried to rest them on the fiberglass side-railing of the boat with our left arm (assuming right-handed operators) across the top to hold them down, on target, while we moved the spray of fire laterally across the target area. This reduced our effective movement to a lateral spread, but in the early models of the weapon it was necessary.

Our accuracy of fire was additionally exacerbated, since we were constantly on the move and generally at a high rate of speed. When we came under fire with a four-man crew, only three men would be manning weapons since one operated the boat. That left one on the front 50, one on the aft 50, and one man firing the M-60. Of course, this was the plan, and as was normally the case in a fight, plans often fell apart, so we shifted fire to whatever worked.

All the crews were pretty adept at figuring out when something was working and when something else was needed, so there was little need for shouted orders. We just grabbed whatever weapon was most appropriate to the situation and hung on until it was over. When someone was wounded or killed, the closest man grabbed his weapon, assuming his had a superior fire-ratio, and continued until the situation had come under control, at which time the wounded man was attended to. PBR crews were known for stability and control in firefights, even when individuals were hit. The four of us, Billy, Jack, David, and I, had worked together often enough that we could sense each other's actions. The more serious the situation became, the more smoothly we worked, almost choreographed in our movements.

The front-fifty gunner, our principle source of firepower, was additionally hampered due to the fact that the bow rose out of the water at high speed, limiting his range of fire. A good boat captain, and Billy was one of the best, used his control of the boat to help the front gunner's accuracy, while at the same time limiting our exposure to return fire through expert maneuvering.

We usually made passes at high speed, traversing a path that gave us the best advantage, exited the area, regrouped, then returned for as many passes as the job required. Our only defense in a firefight was maneuverability. Unlike our enemy, we had no cover and concealment. Operationally, when we were engaged or ambushed, we didn't exit the area. We cleared the range of fire long enough to regroup, but unless we were seriously surprised and overpowered, as was the case when Musetti and Graham were killed, we always went back in and re-engaged until the fight was over

Arriving at the mouth of "Stay-away Straits" that night, we were confronted by total confusion. The confusion was complicated by the fact that our radio communications with the ARVNs had to be filtered through an interpreter.

Tracers were flying from both sides of the canal and in virtually every direction. Enemy tracers, generally Chinese-made, were a slightly different, lighter shade, and often green in color, which gave us a little advantage in terms of fire placement.

Tracer rounds in combat were indispensable, especially at night. When the Douglas AC-47 gunships (codenamed "Puff the Magic Dragon" or "Spooky") were involved in a support capacity, their rate of fire was so high that the fourth-round tracers gave the appearance of a solid string of red descending from the air, gently waving around as it reached out to connect with its intended target on the ground.

The accompanying sound was a continuous, deep, guttural *brrrrrrrrrr* reaching your ears a few seconds after the sight of the red string. The total

AC-47 gunships firing in support during a firefight. Referred to as "Spooky" for their rapid tracer fire, which gave the impression of a magic ray, especially at night.

effect presented an auditory as well as visual metaphor some described as "the Devil, vomiting destruction."

A natural tendency when involved in your first few firefights was to duck as often as possible. Soon, however, everyone came to the realization that this was a futile effort since there was nothing to duck behind; the hull of the boat was fiberglass. Besides, human ducking reflexes wouldn't exactly outpace a bullet. Generally, after a couple of firefights, everyone learned to put their faith in God, maintain as much of a visual of the source of enemy fire as possible, and drive on.

That night, in "Stay-away," we knew which side of the canal the outpost was on, and even though we were drawing fire from that side as well as the opposite bank, we made our first pass, centering a heavy barrage of fire on the opposite side. Return fire subsided momentarily, and Billy took the opportunity to slow our pass speed, allowing us to deliver a heftier punch.

As we exited the fire corridor and spun around, he idled the engines to make sure we were ready for a return pass, like a horse in a medieval battle pausing to catch his breath, stamping the earth impatiently and straining at the bit, before galloping back into the fray.

20. Anatomy of a Firefight

As soon as everyone signaled ready, he throttled up to full speed. The boat reared out of the water like the aforementioned brave stallion, lifting high in the air, and we launched forward. Entry into the fire corridor on the second pass wasn't going to be slow. The enemy was prepared this time and would do one of two things: concentrate heavy fire on us as we passed or retreat back into the jungle.

Under normal circumstance, during the pre–Tet era, we could safely assume the latter, but we had already surmised that Tet was an all-out effort, and retreat would more than likely not be an option the VC and NVA would choose to embrace any time soon. Our firing runs did, however, offer some respite for the outpost defenders, giving them a chance to regroup. This was, after all, our mission.

An hour doesn't seem like a long time for most folks, but an hour spent being shot at on a fairly consistent basis is a virtual eternity. When we finally made a pass and received little to no return fire from the bush, we knew it was over. Our interpreter called the ARVN commander and told him we were heading in to survey the aftermath and assist in any way we could.

It was still dark, and emotions, as they normally are for some time following a good fight, remained high. It would not have been unusual in the dark to trigger some last-minute friendly fire in our direction.

An examination of the boat that night revealed a few holes, but nothing that would hamper our returning to base and refitting. Pure luck and God's grace had decreed once again that on that night, none of us would be wounded. There were multiple ARVN casualties, and we loaded those who could be safely moved and headed back to Sadec. We would return in the light of day to check for enemy KIA, but we didn't expect to find much. Charlie had a systematic, highly efficient process for removing their KIA and WIA to prevent accurate battle assessments.

I was still under the influence of probably pill number two at that time, but it didn't prevent every muscle in my body, tense from the fight, from screaming at me. I spelled Billy at the wheel on the way back in, grinding my teeth from the adrenaline rush.

Upon arrival at home base, a closer examination of the holes in the boat indicated nothing that needed immediate attention. We offloaded the wounded, reloaded and refitted as best we could, and headed back out, just as the horizon was turning a pale grey to signal the new day. There were no kids on the bridge that morning, another indication of our world changing post–Tet.

21

SEAL PBR Operations: Just Do It

The days following Tet were filled with activity. The increased optempo became the norm so that a day without at least one good fight seemed almost eerily suspect, as if God had thrown it in to allow us to "gird our loins" for something more difficult. Slow and uneventful days were rare in the coming weeks and months.

The post–Tet activity brought about a type of routine we were unaccustomed to. Whereas most if not all operations before Tet required two boat patrols, afterwards we found ourselves doing quite a few single-boat ops. We were also tasked with a lot more SEAL and special operations missions.

Virtually all riverine PBR sections were collocated with a SEAL team. Section 513 had one six to ten-man team along with a small "spec ops" support contingency in our compound. The support contingency consisted of a maintenance crew accustomed to the specialized gear the SEAL team used, as well as their own intelligence assets. They received regular intelligence briefs from traditional intelligence sources in Saigon, but the type of operations they ran required a much more "down in the weeds" type of information.

They had their own modified PBR, but it was used most often for snooping around areas they were considering for operations. Once they had a mission in mind, which often took no more than a few hours to conceive, plan, rehearse, and launch, they always called on us to insert them, hang out for fire support, and extract them once their mission had been conducted.

We normally weren't told the mission details unless it was necessary to allow the most advantageous support fire. We would simply be instructed to pick the guys up at the pier. Once on board, they'd point out an insertion point and give us a timeframe to expect a signal for extraction. We'd usually idle in as close as we could to the shore, at low speed for the sake of silence, generally in the darkest part of the night. The team would slip into the water or off the bow of the boat and disappear into the jungle. We'd back off a few hundred yards and maintain position.

If the mission was a capture/kill mission, there would normally be little to no accompanying fire, unless things went awry. We'd simply see a dim light signal for the pickup, move into the same spot onshore, pick up the team and possibly their detainee, and RTB.

Occasionally the team would meet more resistance than expected, in which case they'd radio for fire support and as soon as feasible move themselves to the extraction point. Their ability to coordinate precise fire from our 50s was uncanny. In these instances, it almost seemed that the confusion accompanying typical firefights simply wasn't there. We were pretty good at it, but the SEAL teams were expert at using confusion to their advantage.

The team members were always professional and perfectly organized. They kept pretty much to themselves and of necessity never discussed their missions or mission results with us. When they were on the boats with us, they moved to the rear and stayed there, keeping a low profile while we were operating unless we were still engaged in a fight. If that was the case, they mixed expertly into our movements and joined in.

The teams rotated in and out every few weeks so there was little time to get to know any of them, even if they were more involved with us. On one occasion, however, I had a chance to get to know a member of the team who was from a neighborhood close to home in central Mississippi.

He was a wiry-built kid named Gary Hux. Like most of the young SEALs, he wasn't muscle bound. They were more like bull riders: wiry and slim. Gary had gone to the same high school I attended and was two years ahead of me. He'd joined the Navy soon after graduating, finished basic training, and was immediately recruited into the Underwater Demolition Team (UDT), the forerunner of the Navy SEAL teams.

During downtimes, we just talked about home over warm beer in the makeshift bar on the compound. We talked about girls, loves lost and gained, family, and all the things in our lives that had gone into the wide end of the funnel and helped to spit us out the narrow end, at this place and time. It was a great stress reliever, talking about home with someone who knew "home."

We were amazed to find out we even had some of the same teachers in high school.

"Did you have ol' Mrs. Alexander for English?" Gary asked me one evening.

"Yeah, I replied. "Hell, I think everybody in Jackson, Mississippi, knew Mrs. Alexander. I always felt a little sorry for her though. Guys used to play tricks on her all the time."

"Yeah," he laughed. "I remember one time it started raining, and one of the guys asked her if he could go roll up the windows on his car. She said, 'Yeah, go ahead.' Another one of my buddies piped up and said, 'Mrs. Alexander, can I go out and roll the windows up on my motorcycle?' She said, 'Yeah, go ahead,' and when everybody cracked up as the guy walked out of the classroom, she said, 'He ain't foolin' me. He probably doesn't even have a motorcycle.'"

Talking about things like this, in a place where there were so many life and death things to talk about, seemed like a spiritual process; it was as if we had surpassed death and dying, looked back and sniffed at them, choosing to elevate all the mundane into nobler narratives about Ms. Alexander and such.

As much as I had wanted to know about Gary's SEAL training and what it was like to be one of the best, it just seemed more important to me to talk about ol' Mrs. Alexander and girls at Central High School. He agreed.

One evening a week after Tet, close to midnight, we had been on patrol for an hour or so when we got a call to RTB and pick up the team. Back at base, we found the guys painted up, geared up, and waiting for us at the pier. Gary nodded at me and tipped his right index finger off the edge of his cap in my direction as if to say, "That's just about all the talking we're gonna have time to do tonight."

The team leader spoke to Billy, pointed on the map to a small inlet off one of the main canals south of us, and we headed out. There was nothing much more to discuss as we all knew the drill. They had jumped aboard, indicated the insertion point, and settled into the rear of the boat in less than two minutes as we headed toward the drop off point.

The insertion went smoothly, and as usual, once the last man had stepped off the boat, the entire team disappeared into the jungle as if absorbed by the foliage. We backed off and idled about a hundred yards into the main river. Twenty minutes later a serious firefight erupted in the area where the team had been inserted. We were called to make a high-speed run to their south, providing as much fire as possible behind them.

They marked the enemy location with red tracer heavy automatic fire and flares, but we had no problem spotting Charlie since their fire was laced with bright green tracers. Sporadic grenades exploded in the area where the team was located, indicating a possible forward movement by the enemy element. When an enemy unit intended to advance on their opponent, they often used grenades to soften them up.

We made another run and positioned our boat forward of the team location, which happened to be a hundred yards off the bank, back in the thick jungle, and provided as much concentrated fire as possible into the origins of the green tracer rounds. The team took the opportunity to move parallel to the bank closest to the boat, in a direction away from the enemy, until they closed the distance between us and got close enough to signal for a pickup.

Billy made one last high-speed move parallel to the bank toward the enemy position as we continued laying down a blanket of fire. As the enemy force's fire subsided, no doubt sheltering from our suppressive run, Billy executed a perfect 180, back toward the projected pickup point. In less than 20 seconds, he had brushed up against the thick foliage lining the bank, slowed just enough to allow the team to slip onboard, and cut back to the right. As he throttled full forward on both engines, the bow leaped out of the water, the stern dug in, and we sped out toward the middle of the main river.

The enemy fire shifted in our direction but soon died away as we put more distance between us and the bank, continuing out into the river. Soon we were out of range, and Billy reduced to cruising speed heading back to Sadec. Spotting Gary crouched in the corner at the rear of the boat wiping at the camo on his face, I knelt down and patted him on the shoulder, chuckling.

"Damn man, that must have been a hell of a hornet's nest y'all stepped into," I laughed.

As it was still dark, I didn't have a clear view of his face, but I could see a smile anyhow. His white teeth were glowing through the sweat, camo paint, residue from gun powder, and splashes of drying mud. He looked at me and wiped across his forehead with a dirty green cloth. As he did so, I saw traces of blood and a huge bump the size of a golf ball inching out just below his hairline. It was at that point I noticed his hands visibly shaking as he wiped his forehead again and winced slightly at the pain. In spite of this, he was still smiling.

"What the fuck, Gary. You okay, man?" I asked.

"Yeah," he replied. "You ain't gonna believe this shit."

"Were you guys hand to hand in there?" I continued before he had time to explain. "Looks like somebody smacked you in the head pretty hard. Didn't seem like you were that close in on each other."

He chuckled at this, and the effort caused him to wince.

"No man, that's the crazy part. I got hit in the head with a damn grenade, a fucking grenade. Can you believe that shit? Hit smack in the forehead with a damn grenade." Slight nervous twitches entered his tone, mixed with the still persistent giggling.

I just looked at him, trying to form a visual of what he had said, my mouth open in disbelief.

"Damn thing just smacked the shit out of me and fell right at my feet. Nothing I could do but wait," he continued. "It happened so fast I couldn't even think to try and kick it away or pick it up. I just stood there, saying a short prayer and waiting. Hit hard enough to damn near knock me unconscious. It was like getting hit in a baseball game."

"You're kidding. Why, I mean, what the hell happened?" I asked.

"That's it," he continued, still wiping his face more gently now. "Nothing happened. It just dropped and laid there."

Then it hit me. Several weeks before, we had uncovered a small shipment of ammo and grenades hidden in some old wooden crates being transported on the river. Mixed in the shipment were several homemade booby-trap land mines. The grenades too were homemade. They were made from beer cans packed with explosives and a crude timing detonator. Some had no timer at all. They were designed to detonate as soon as the clip was snatched off, no doubt by a hidden trip wire. An ingenious wooden handle was molded onto the top of the timed ones in order to facilitate throwing.

"Son of a bitch," I said. "It was a dud, huh?"

"Good Lord must have something else planned for me," Gary continued, still shaking slightly.

"Fuckin-A!" I added. It was a short but emphatic expression of agreement often used by the guys back home. For two Mississippi boys, no further elaboration was necessary.

22

OCCASIONALLY OUT
OF THE BUSH

A few years after the Vietnam war had ended, Francis Ford Coppola directed the famous movie, *Apocalypse Now*, focusing on a fictional renegade colonel. In the film, Colonel Walter Kurtz went rogue and took his loyal Montagnard troops into the mountains from whence he launched his own little war on the Vietcong and NVA. The public response seemed to be that, though it was an entertaining film, such a thing could never have happened during the war.

In point of fact, though an actual renegade officer on a par with Colonel Kurtz never existed, rogue operations and rogue operators following Tet were not only around, they sometimes seemed more plentiful than traditional units.

The Tet offensive was so unexpected and caused so much chaos among war planners all the way up to General Westmoreland's Military Assistance Command, Vietnam (MACV), many smaller unit organizations were left to formulate and conduct operations independent of higher coordination.

SEAL teams and Army Special Forces teams throughout the country had, even prior to Tet, been fairly independent in operational planning, but in the aftermath of Tet, many saw a situation in which C&C (command and control) shifted from Saigon down to the ground level special operations planners. It was not unusual for these guys to be sitting around drinking beer when one would pop off with, "Hey man, what would you think about us doing X or Y? Wouldn't that be a hoot?"

If something seemed like a good idea to them, they just did it. There may have been some coordination for air support, but for most of the special operations community in country on the heels of Tet, a mission would be conceived in the morning and launched that afternoon or night. Section 513's SEAL support activity, as well as that of most of the PBR

Preparing for a post–Tet operation by South Vietnamese Special Forces. PBRs often inserted and extracted these operators, as well as provided support fire from offshore when needed.

sections throughout country, was in high gear for weeks in the first quarter of 1968.

Increased "spook" operations, as we affectionately referred to them, became the norm, and this included a class of operator that fell somewhere between legitimate and non-existent. The intelligence gatherer in country, the Central Intelligence Agency (CIA), was joined in its offensive intelligence operations against the north by intelligence agencies from several other countries, and they were not necessarily always on the same page.

The function of intelligence field operators is to coordinate the activity of a group of people who gather information for them, collect from these gatherers, then pass that information on to the appropriate command levels. Occasionally in those days, they would simply cut out the middle man, obtain the information, and launch their own operations.

The post–Tet chaos and confusion seemed to green-light as much of this activity as individual intelligence operators desired to undertake. Therefore, if intelligence gatherers reported that some village official was cooperating with the enemy, the intel officers themselves would simply plan a kill mission or DACK (direct action capture/kill) using their locals, and go take the guy out.

As long as the ends were met, the means were rarely questioned. Of course, many analysts agree, it was just such an attitude that created an atmosphere which allowed extremely rare incidents to occur such as that which happened in My Lai in March of that year. This loose war footing and command chaos could be seen all the way up the chain, even in DC, and seemed to green-light an inordinate amount of freelancing.

Special operators such as Special Forces and SEAL teams were comfortable with this type of warfare, but as professionals, they didn't allow it to get out of control. For young folks thrown into this arena and told to do "that which is necessary to get the job done," however, things often got dicey.

For us, even though we were called on to support such operations, even in the post–Tet atmosphere, our command never allowed us to be hung out. Other than my SEAL friend Gary, we had little personal contact with individuals who operated almost entirely "in the bush."

Throughout Vietnam, there was a class of soldier/civilian operator who rarely came in from the thickest parts of the jungle. These individuals saw a burst of usefulness and utilization during this post–Tet period.

One such individual, an Australian operating in and around the jungles between our location and Saigon, occasionally visited our compound to shower, eat a hot meal or two, share some intelligence with our command, and re-supply himself and his native companions. As if by magic, he would simply appear on the edge of the compound with half a dozen natives, stroll into a secure area of the compound that was kept open for him, and do his thing for a day or so. Then, along with his men, he would step to the same edge of the compound and disappear again.

His visits became much more frequent after Tet, and he became more open and talkative. He happened to have spent some time in the Birmingham, Alabama, area before the war, close to where Billy grew up. Jack, David, and Billy often drank a beer or two with him at the bami-bar in town.

He probably felt comfortable with them because they never asked him what he did. By that time, so many people in Vietnam did so many weird things in pursuit of the war effort, we became blasé about the topic. Still it must have been nice for him to know he could relax, drink a few beers with some ol' Southern boys, and just unwind a bit.

Then one day, for some reason, that changed. As they talked over an ice-cube and sawdust chip-filled glass of beer, he suddenly became chatty about his role.

"There are some people on the periphery of the war here who aren't really bad, but they sure as hell ain't good. Know what I mean, mate?" he mused nonchalantly, while maneuvering a somewhat larger than normal piece of wood out of his glass with a pinky finger.

"You guys can't afford to take them out due to their status, but none of us can afford to allow them to do what they're doing. Somebody has to engage them, try and convince them legitimately to mend their ways, or..." Here he paused and gazed off at the clouds in the sky with a squint, as if searching for the right words. "I don't know; deal with them I guess."

"You don't have to explain anything to us," David offered. "We're glad you're out there, and I would imagine you're glad we're here. Mate," he added with a smile.

He grinned a most sincere grin and took a big swig of beer.

"Tell you what, though," Billy chimed in. "I've always been curious as to how you get along when you're out there. I mean, I know your guys over there," he added, swinging a thumb back toward the security entrance to the compound, "are great to have around, but you don't have a lot of back-up if things get bad."

The Australian rubbed his chin a minute and said, "So, you mean you think it may be worse out there for me than in here for you?"

"Actually, I'm sort of joking," he continued, "but the fact is, I think about you guys now and then, out there on the river. In so many ways, I have a lot more security. I speak all the dialects pretty well, and those guys I move with are my friends, just like y'all are friends. We're devoted to each other and to what we do, just like y'all are. Besides, I'm always pretty close to some installation, whether it's ours or the ARVNs."

He took another drink and continued, "There's a lot of folks out there in the bush who do similar things, either on or off the books. Hell of a lot of it more off than on lately," he added as an afterthought. "We sort of network now and then."

"Yeah," David offered, "something else I've noticed about you 'bush guys' too; you don't ever seem to get that 'hundred-mile' stare. You know, that weary look that a lot of the guys get when they're just tired of it all."

"Maybe I don't ever get tired of it," he said. "I don't know. I guess I sort of try to think like an animal sometimes, just going about my day and doing this because I have to do it to survive and doing that because I have to do it to survive."

22. Occasionally Out of the Bush

"My friends over there," he nodded in the direction of a group of his Montagnard compatriots, patiently sitting and talking among themselves like they may have been out on their back porch watching the sun set, "are pretty sophisticated in their world, you know, but they don't know they're missing out on color TV or fried chicken. Hell, I'm not even sure they know they're going to die one day."

"You know," he turned suddenly toward David as if he'd just thought of something important, "human beings are the only species blessed, or cursed, depending on how you look at it, with the knowledge of their own mortality. When an animal, like a water buffalo for instance, loses a young one, he doesn't mourn or anything. He probably just figures the young one never was there in the first place or something."

He paused, shook his head thoughtfully, and continued, "Seems like from a very early age, we humans know that one day we won't be here anymore, and we spend the rest of our lives trying to cram as much as we can into this short space in time, and it's never enough. We always die sad, feeling we missed out on something. I've tried to think like the water buffalo. My friends over there have already achieved that goal. Some of it rubs off on me when we're out in the bush."

A long pause ensued, everyone taking deep drinks from their beer, not knowing what to say. Finally, Billy chimed in, as only Billy could have. "So, how's the weather this time of year back where you're from?"

Once the laughter subsided, he went on to explain that that very evening, he and his guys would meet with a local village official a few klicks north, and that, though he didn't know it yet, the man would have an opportunity to make a life-altering decision that very evening. He'd either provide some valuable information about a Vietcong element he had been collecting village taxes to support and leave the area for good, or he'd "have the opportunity to uncover the answer to life's most important question."

"You mean, 'Are grandma and grandpa really waiting for us on the other side?'" Billy chuckled.

"Hell, I hope not," David added. "I mean... Never mind."

As if on cue, his four friends wandered up, their gear packed and ready, and handed a pack and weapon to him. He finished his beer, nodded to the guys, and said, "I should be back around in a few days. We'll pick up there, hopefully."

That was the last time he and his men made it into the compound. We talked about it one evening, wondering where he was, but were unwilling to ask our intel guys. Sometimes you're better off assuming the answer to a question than actually verifying one way or the other. Besides, folks were relocating much more frequently in those days, and when that happened, it wasn't unusual to lose touch completely.

23

THE MEDICINE WAS
DEFINITELY WORSE

There were only two people we could be certain of seeing on a fairly regular basis, both pre– and post–Tet. The first was the guy who showed up on a chopper every month to pay us. The second was the medic who flew in regularly to stick a "ten penny"–sized needle filled with gamma globulin—a vaccine that was more paste than fluid—in our butts. I never could understand how we were not eligible for a Purple Heart for having been wounded by that guy every two months.

I was fortunate, and blessed, not to have been wounded while in country, but Jack and several other guys who had been swore that being wounded by an AK-47 5.56mm round was less painful than the bi-monthly shot. The solution was thick and cold, and once it was injected into your hip, it sat there and burned for what seemed like hours.

Unlike the medic, we all looked forward to the pay chopper, even though there was really no place to spend the little bit of pay we received. Billy, Jack, David, and I were all the same rank. We earned around $430 a month but had a large amount of that sent home before payment in the form of annuities or savings bonds or something, just to give us a little nest egg. In Vietnam we were paid the remainder in MPC (military payment certificate) in denominations ranging from 50 cents to $20. We called it Monopoly money because that's exactly what it looked like.

It was pretty much worthless in the local economy. The locals couldn't exchange MPC for Vietnamese currency or American dollars. If we wanted to spend money at the bami-bar or the Golden Gate (the finest house of prostitution in Vietnam, located on the outskirts of Sadec), we had to exchange our MPC for Vietnamese currency at a U.S.-managed exchange facility, and they were primarily located at large installations such as those found in Saigon.

Brothers in the Mekong Delta

If you already had American currency, the locals would exchange it in town for Vietnamese currency. Unfortunately for us, the exchange of dollars for Vietnamese currency was illegal, or at least against military regulations. It was against regulations because American currency was worth a lot more than Vietnamese currency, and when Vietnamese money changers got hold of it, it was often funneled into enemy coffers.

More than one enterprising American serviceman had U.S. currency sent to him on a regular basis in simple envelopes through the mail, exchanged it on the local market for much more cash value in Vietnamese currency. He hoarded all of it while in country, then exchanged the Vietnamese currency back into U.S. greenbacks when he departed, gambling of course, that he would depart alive. All life was a gamble in Vietnam.

Most of us, however, were ignorant of all the economic variances and inconsistencies. All we knew was that the MPC guy showed up on time, and the only place we could spend the money was in our little make-shift bar on compound: 15 cents for a beer and 25 cents for a shot of whiskey. A quart went for anywhere from $2 to $7. America didn't send fifths to Vietnam. Before we left Vietnam, most of us had forgotten what an actual fifth of whiskey even looked like.

You could get a shot of local whiskey at the bami-bar in town but it was rice whiskey. Though I eventually prided myself to be a "hard drinker," I couldn't handle it. I've never drunk gasoline, but in describing it, that's the best comparison I can make. Billy and Jack, however, were better at most everything than I was, including drinking the local rice whiskey.

Once, on a day off in town on a "committed, drunken tear," David and I had determined to break through that "burning throat" barrier and become seasoned rice whiskey imbibers like Billy and Jack. Neither of us managed to make it, though David did try harder. We finally decided to call it a day and headed back just before dark.

Back at the compound, Billy and Jack poured the protesting David onto his cot, all the while teasing him because he couldn't handle it. Presumably I was next in line for the ribbing once David had passed out. David spent the next 30 minutes or so alternately passing out and then waking, determined to go back to the bar for more rice whiskey. Between bouts of laughter and teasing, Billy and Jack just held him down.

Eventually tiring of keeping him on his cot and ready to pass out themselves, they decided the best thing to do was to tie him down. They didn't have rope, but there were several rolls of "hundred mile an hour" tape (duct tape, affectionately dubbed such because it could hold a jeep together at speeds of 100 miles an hour).

Five minutes later, David lay taped securely to his bed. They even taped his mouth so they wouldn't have to listen to his protests during those brief moments of lucidity he'd demonstrated. Finally, the three of us fell onto our own racks and drifted off.

In later discussions, we never determined exactly how long we were out before the attack warning sounded. Similar to a general quarters alarm, the alarm would sound when we were being targeted by mortars or an all-out manned assault, and everyone in the compound would rush out to pre-designated fighting positions.

When the alarm sounded early that morning, in our haste and as a result of the drunken state we were still experiencing, we forgot David. Fortunately, he never woke up. In hindsight, we consoled ourselves that he was probably in the safest place, neatly taped to his cot. Though he chided us, we took solace in pointing out that we had put so much tape around him that it far surpassed any protection he would have had from a flak jacket.

Though not necessarily equal to Christmas morning, we usually looked forward to the payday chopper's visit. In contrast, the chopper bringing the medic and the "ten-penny nail"–needles loaded with Vaseline was on par with a Monday morning following the best weekend of your life on which you had to get out of bed with a really bad hangover and go to work at the very worst job imaginable.

On medic days, if there was a dangerous mission on tap forecasting an extremely high casualty rate, people stood in line to volunteer for it. And as macho and determined as Jack was, he, David, Billy, and I were normally first in line. The utmost valor and courage were not even close enough to prepare one for those shots. Grown men quaked at the site of that chopper.

We used to joke that the government "mad scientists" were experimenting with a new strain of gamma globulin that they hoped would cure cancer. Section 513 guys were the chosen guinea pigs. This new strain was the consistency of play dough, hence the huge needles needed to inject it. It had to be really cold when injected too. Once injected, it took what seemed like an hour to seep into the blood stream, during which time it just sat there and burned.

"They'll probably kill a few of us before they get that 'cancer cure,'" Billy joked one day as we stood in line to volunteer for a DACK mission due to kick off the evening before the "gamma globulin guy" arrived, "but hell, it'll make a real man out of you, huh."

In reality, gamma globulin is an antibiotic vaccine that protects against all types of harmful bacteria, and Vietnam was replete with harmful bacteria. Unfortunately, many young folks in that country died or were seriously impaired, not by bullets or shrapnel, but by some tiny organism they either inhaled or accidentally ingested.

Once, on a hastily organized mission to recover the crew of a downed chopper, I stepped on a bamboo shoot that caused a minor cut on my heel. The dozens of vials of gamma globulin that had been injected into my ass over the months were supposed to have protected me from infection, but they didn't.

Though it didn't keep me from patrol duties, my foot became infected, and the infection seemed incurable the rest of my time in Vietnam. The gamma globulin injections didn't prevent it, and though the medics were all professional and committed, they couldn't get rid of it. When you were tagged with an infection in Vietnam, it was like getting a tattoo; the only way to get rid of it was to cut off that particular body part. I chose to live with it and douse it with iodine now and then.

Months later, on my return to America, I was blessed to have the opportunity to live with Jack's family for a while. Vance Anderson, Jack's dad and the only father figure I ever had in my life since my own died when I was a baby, took pains to dress my infection every day with some old farmer's concoction he'd known about all his life. Every day for weeks, he'd gently take my foot in his lap and, just as gently, remove the bandage he'd placed there the day before, reapply the concoction, and re-bandage it. One day, the infection was gone.

We lose sight of the fact that we have to experience a lot of pain now and then so we can experience the joy that follows. One of the most pleasant feelings a person can have is the feeling of pain easing off after you've hit your thumb with a hammer, and it finally begins to stop hurting so bad. The problem with that is that the only way you can ever experience that amazing feeling is to hit your thumb with a hammer. The mysterious ways in which God works brought many wonderful people and amazing experiences into my life, but I'll always put Jack's dad, Vance, at the top of the list.

24

A Most
Well-known Monkey

The Tet offensive, in actuality, had been a dismal failure for the north. NVA military planners and strategists had envisioned several victorious battles which would result in the NVA occupation of key areas of Saigon and pivotal cities such as Hue, all of which would be followed by a popular uprising among the people of South Vietnam in favor of the north. None of this happened. What did happen, however, was a drastic operational change on the part of MACV (Military Assistance Command, Vietnam), and of course, a more rapidly deteriorating atmosphere of support among the American people.

As for 513, we eventually got back to a somewhat normal operational tempo. We stayed on a 12 and 12 schedule of patrols and never really got back to that push-pull feel of the war. Rather than the pre–Tet checkers game tempo that we had felt would go on forever, there now seemed to be a constant feeling of moving at a higher rate of speed toward an end. We did resume normal two-boat patrols and playing "cop" on the river mixed with a higher number of standard operational missions and SEAL forays.

There also seemed to be an increased number of firefights than that which we had experienced before Tet, but even that became part of the norm for us. The short of it was, we began to relax a little more and focus a bit more on the humor of Vietnam and the war. There was plenty of that, like the incident with Ho Chi Minh, the pet monkey.

One of the Vinh Long boat crews had adopted and somewhat domesticated a Capuchin monkey, though we always questioned who domesticated whom. The monkey, affectionately dubbed "Ho" for Ho Chi Minh, lived on the boat and went on patrol with the crew. He eventually became a virtually unseen member of the crew once the novelty had passed, and remained so until one day in early spring. On that day, Ho became famous among PBR sections throughout the country.

Brothers in the Mekong Delta

Every boat crew had good luck rituals they followed and bad luck rituals they avoided, some particular to that specific crew and some observed by every PBR section in the country. One of the good luck rituals observed by almost every section was keeping the ring pins from the grenades that were thrown in firefights.

The ring pin is the device on a grenade which, when pulled, allowed the firing sequence to initiate. The grenades we used in Vietnam didn't have a safety clip on them because it required an extra step in arming the grenade. We routinely removed them from grenades we stored close to the front gunner position for use in firefights, so the only safety was the pin itself. From the pulling of the pin and the release of the "spoon" lever, a grenade would explode in approximately four seconds unless it malfunctioned (which was not unusual), in which case the timing would be slowed, or the grenade might not explode at all.

The ritual required keeping only the pins from grenades actually used in firefights, not the ones thrown to stun fish for the locals or simply to break the monotony of a slow day. A large collection of ring pins signified a patrol crew that had experienced a large number of close quarter fights, since grenades were generally used in fights that had become heated.

To understand clearly the events of the day that Ho the monkey became famous, you must picture the front gun tub from which the forward, twin 50s were operated. The front gunner kept four or five live grenades hung by the "pin-secured" handle on one the side of the tub. On the other side, he kept the aforementioned used rings, usually in a small can of sorts.

One slow day in late March, our patrol met up with the Vinh Long crew, of which Ho was a member. We maneuvered out into the middle of the river as far from either bank as possible, and tied our four boats together, cutting the engines.

As it was a beautiful day, we gathered on Ho's boat toward the stern to just sit, relax, catch up on war news or news of common friends, and laugh at the antics of the monkey as he jumped around and scratched his ass, enjoying the attention.

All told, there were eight of us sitting on the sides of the boat or engine cover or just standing around idly chatting. We had drifted for approximately 15 minutes, watching as Ho leapt around, chirping and grinning. He would disappear for a moment and then surface in another area of the boat with a favorite toy, showing off for us.

At one point, he jumped across the boat and disappeared up toward the bow. We ignored him and continued with our gossip. Then the following event occurred, absent supporting verbal communication from any of us. There was no need for words in this instance. This was one of those occasions when human beings communicate expertly with eye contact and facial expression alone.

Ho, a look of mystery and pride on his little monkey face, swung cheerily around the corner of the boat, coming from the direction of the gun tub and swinging on his little monkey index finger a grenade pin. If he could have whistled, he would have resembled, in every aspect, some guy strolling down a sidewalk in the city, whistling and twirling his car keys.

The potential implications of such a sight formed and projected from one mind to the next in less than a millisecond. Before we knew it, we all found ourselves in the water, alternately ducking under the surface, and rising with our hands over our ears. In perfect unison, we all had determined that discretion was the better part of valor—valor in this case entailed gambling that Ho had simply picked up a used pin and not actually pulled one from a live grenade.

The only living creature on the four boats was Ho, who seemed completely perplexed and somewhat amused at the antics of his human counterparts.

25

THE "RIGHT"
AND THE "GOOD"

Vietnam, for so many of us, was a time as well as a place. As a whole, the year or more that individuals spent there was a single point in the timeline of their lives, much the same as a first love or a first kiss. It was also important because, though a single time, it was filled with a multitude of smaller pivotal, life-altering events, like a cell containing a multitude of smaller cells.

Some of these events lasted mere seconds, but they were so profound, they would mark turning points in individual lives, creating the kind of memories that would haunt. These were the memories that would sneak back into a man's consciousness periodically throughout the remainder of his days, triggered by a smell or a sound or a feeling from just the right breeze blowing across his face.

Less than a week in country, I dropped by our makeshift bar one evening to pick up a few beers on my way back to our tent following a patrol. Several groups were scattered around the place, drinking and talking louder than necessary, the way men will when they're tight.

"Do you think we'll ever be forgiven for some of the stuff we done?" someone asked, though I couldn't tell whether he was asking himself or the guy sitting next to him at the table. He had a strong drawl that reminded me of home, and as such drew my attention to a conversation of which I was not a part. The question I'd overheard, rhetorical as it may have been, was just loud enough to reach my passing ear.

I picked up four beers, holding two in my left hand, securing one under my armpit, and grabbing the fourth with my other hand. As I turned to leave, I glanced at him. The look on his face was blank, expressionless and bland, as if he was intentionally phasing out any emotion that would normally accompany such a question. Just before I turned away, I thought I saw a hint of fear in him.

25. The "Right" and the "Good"

When I got back to the tent, I slipped my boots off, and pierced the top of one of my beers with the opener I kept hanging on the bed frame. The tent was empty. I sat on the edge of my bunk and sipped the lukewarm brew, the question rolling through my mind; *"Do you think we'll ever be forgiven?"*

I took another long, deep pull from the beer as I thought about the question and why it was important enough to him to be voiced aloud. Maybe he and his friend had done something bad. Maybe he was talking about some isolated incident. "Maybe," I mused, "maybe he was just speaking in generalities, waxing philosophical, the way men will do when they drink."

Something bothered me though. An unsettling feeling came over me, one of those feelings that brings you down without explaining why. Suddenly, it hit me: the why. The unsettling feeling I had was because I realized that the "we" he was talking about included me.

I was the new guy. I had yet to even conceive of the "things" he was talking about. They were yet to come for me, but somehow, I felt they were preordained, inescapable. I felt like Ebenezer Scrooge, kneeling before my own headstone. At the same time, I had a premonition that the forgiveness I would one day seek was not going to be for drinking too much or forgetting to write home. The look on his face was proof of that.

That day and today and all the days that have passed between them, I understand perfectly why the guy in the bar asked the question. I was honest and upright in all that I did. Jack and Billy and David and the rest of us were all honest and honorable in our actions. Every service member, before departing the States for Vietnam, was given a small card with the words "Code of Conduct" emblazoned on the face of it. The instructions on back began, "I am an American fighting man..." These words preceded a set of pledges we made to the people of America.

The card was official. It came from the highest level of command in our nation. For us, simple, rough around the edges, uneducated, barely out of high school kids, it was like being given the original tablets upon which the Ten Commandments were inscribed. Whether we admitted it or not, that simple little card was special, almost regal in nature. I have mine still today.

Reading over these words now makes me feel like a hero. They meant so much to me and to us all; we prided ourselves on the things the words represented. And though we all kept the pledge in our hearts, Vietnam was a place where it was almost impossible to live up to the words inscribed on that little card. And today, still today at 72 years of age, not a week goes by in which I don't ask for forgiveness, the forgiveness of which my nameless friend spoke, and the peace it might bring.

Vietnam vets—the ones who've been involved in combat—never ask each other to talk about the ghosts they carry with them. It's not a matter of politeness or secrecy; it's just that everyone is dealing with those isolated incidents, the times they had to do that which was right instead of that which was good.

The "right" was operational, expedient. The "right" was what the war effort required. It was what had to be done to win. It was that thing you had to wince a little to do. It was passing by a young man, hands tied behind him, blindfolded, bent over at the waist under a barbed wire enclosure that scored his back each time he moved so much as an inch, and pretending that you hadn't noticed it.

"Right" was also expedient. It didn't require a lot of thought, and in war, thought is what kills you and your brothers. As a matter of fact, doing the "right" was what you were trained for and, in most cases, you were trained to do it instinctively and without contemplation. The problem, however, was that the contemplation always came. It came later, but it always came. When it came, you dealt with it by rationalizing. It was a never-ending process, one in which you would engage for the rest of your days; first the memory, clear and distinct, then the rationalizing, in the futile hope that your rationalization would end the cycle. If you could just justify what happened, just once, you'd never have to take part in such an effort again.

To be fair, the "right" was necessary. It was an act committed without moral considerations. It was instinct, and wars could never be won without it. In its most simplistic state, it was pulling the trigger on an individual you had never met and had no real qualitative reason to hate, other than that which you had been told. It was the "right" as opposed to the "good."

Tagging these things with the label "right" was the military's way of blessing the actions, as with the sign of the cross. It has always been assumed that such blessings eliminated any need for later contemplation.

I've been more fortunate than most combat veterans. Over the years I have spent very little time reliving and pondering most of the "right" things I did in Vietnam. As a matter of fact, I am proud of them. They were things that had to be done, and with the help of my brothers, Jack, Billy, David and Phil and all the others, I did them well. We all did them well, and when it comes time to rationalize, in order to be fair with ourselves, that fact has to be included in the mix.

25. The "Right" and the "Good"

It's just those few, rare, "right" things that were not cleansed by the sign of the cross. We all had them. They come to visit us now and then after all these years, and likely will until we rest for that last time. Doing that which was "right," I have come to realize, was the "thing" my nameless friend in the bar that evening wondered if we'd ever be forgiven for.

Those of us on a combat status in Vietnam were very familiar with the "right" as opposed to the "good." Trained to react at all costs, with no consideration whatsoever for contemplation or thought for implications, absent the obvious responses to being shot at, we reacted to situations based on intelligence or directives: this village harbors VC, or this family has sent sons north to fight for Ho, or this person is a direct pipeline to the NVA or a VC tax collector.

Our enemies, other than the obvious—the shooters—were identified for us by people who knew more than we did. Since the Vietnam war was the first extended conflict for the youth of America in which the enemy was totally indistinguishable from the ally, such external identification was necessary. We were told this guy is good; this guy is bad; we like him; we hate him. We had faith in these distinctions, and we didn't question them.

We also acted based on these distinctions and identifications. Such action was, we concluded, "right" even if it was not necessarily "good." It was okay for us, because the "right" was all we needed. We destroyed the rice harvest of an entire village because it was "right." We slaughtered pigs or old, frail, virtually featherless chickens because the people who owned these animals were feeding the enemy. It was "right."

In our commitment to defeating Communism, we did the "right" without question. We accepted it. Only occasionally, while we were there in that time and place, did we ever question it, like when we fired warning shots at boats that were taking evasive actions to avoid being searched and inadvertently hit one of the occupants with an errant round. Then we became like my unidentified friend at the bar, musing over the availability of forgiveness.

We rarely had to ask such questions because it was just too easy to accept the instructions we were given by those who knew. This person deserved to die because of this or that. That family or that village had no right to the crops they'd raised or the animals they'd nurtured because of this or that. We just accepted it. At the time it was easy. It was "right." Some "rights," however, were harder than others to simply leave behind. And some are still with us today.

Every combat veteran of Vietnam, every soldier who took part in firefights on a regular basis, will recall a multitude of singular events, but they all have one particular action that hangs on like a dream. And like a dream, we often relive it, trying to pick it apart and even manipulate it to balance it out, the way one would watch a movie over and over again, subconsciously trying to change the ending.

We remember these events inaccurately. It is impossible to remember them precisely, and often we don't really want to. My "right" came shortly before noon on Sunday, the first week of February 1968.

Our patrol began that morning before sunrise, and as noon approached, the temperature had risen, nearing the high for the day. Traffic on the river had been light all day. The crew had resigned itself to simply riding out the rest of the patrol, trying to stay moderately cool.

Most of the boat captains were relaxed about uniform requirements. Our crew usually wore cutoff uniform pants, t-shirts, and sandals, especially in the hottest part of the day. We kept our flak vests handy, however. PBR crews were not trained in infantry tactics or operations and rarely left the boats during patrols, so the relaxed dress standards made perfect sense.

Every PBR section, 513 included, was assigned a Seawolf crew consisting of two UH-1B Huey helicopter gunships. Their purpose was CAS (close air support) for the boat crews. Available 24 hours a day, they could be airborne and on station within minutes. Armed with door guns and rockets, they were indispensable to us.

As we drifted close to the shore of the Mekong that morning, drowsy from the noonday heat, we took a couple of sniper rounds from the shore. The ineffectiveness of the fire, the rounds splashing in well short of the boat, was such that we didn't take evasive action or even return fire. There were a couple of villages in the area that had been identified by intelligence as predominantly VC supportive, so we figured they were bored and decided to launch a couple of rounds our way.

"Wanna make a run that direction?" Bill Fuller asked.

Bill was at the helm at the moment and instinctively reached for his vest, expecting an order to head closer toward the shore so we could make a couple of firing runs in the general direction of the sniper fire.

"Not much use," boat captain Don Rogers replied. "Tell you what, though. Seawolves haven't been too active the last couple of days. Let's see if they want to make a run on the area."

Bill radioed in to base requesting a firing run, and gave the general coordinates, indicating the only action was a couple of rounds of sniper fire. His call had been more of an offer of activity rather than an urgent call for CAS.

"Sure," came the response from the Seawolf crew member who picked up the call. "We need to get in the air a little today anyhow."

With that, Bill fired the engines and moved out a little further into the center of the river, and we waited for the action to begin. Within minutes two gunships were on station, circling at an altitude of about 1500 feet.

"You're pretty much on top of the area now," Don advised the lead chopper pilot.

"Roger," came the reply.

Our communications were on the same frequency as that of the gunships so we could monitor the ship-to-ship traffic as they prepared to make their run. Watching them make their run prep was nothing new to us. Being tied in on communication and operations with CAS so that we could hear their back and forth, and they ours, was also normal procedure. We kicked back and settled in to enjoy the show, as if we were at a daytime drive-in movie theater.

Suddenly, as if in a dream, the normal, routine, and mundane turned to surreal. The unbelievable was a fairly regular occurrence in Vietnam. However, every now and then something happened that was so outrageous, like watching a plane crash to Earth in your own backyard, that it stretched credulity to the point that all you could do was watch until seconds passed, and your brain had a chance to catch up with your senses.

As the two choppers circled, still at 1300 to 1500 feet, the pilots conversing in normal operational tones, we could see the lead chopper's main rotor begin to slow. At first it was barely noticeable; the blurring of the blade as it rotated slowly became a distinct outline of the actual blades themselves as they whipped around, slower and slower.

We glanced blankly at each other, asking silently if our eyes were playing tricks, refusing to acknowledge what we were seeing. The normal chatter between pilots continued while this was happening until suddenly, for a split second, the radio traffic stopped, then all hell broke loose in their communications.

Frantic radio communication commenced between the copilots of each helicopter, one talking over another. Then all was eerily quiet for another second that seemed like an eternity. Finally, the silence was broken, and we listened as the last words ever spoken by the copilot of the lead chopper came across the air. "*Oh, shit.*" It wasn't a shout or a plea for help. It wasn't even urgent. It was just two words, spoken in a surprisingly calm voice that seemed appropriate at the time and under the circumstances.

As if on cue, the chopper fell from the sky. It didn't flip over or careen wildly from side to side; it just fell gracefully, straight toward the ground. The fall took no more than seconds before it disappeared into the tree line, but it seemed to fall for a long time, in slow motion. It was like watching a movie of a leaf drifting gracefully to the ground.

When I dream about this moment, the events of that day always beginning with the sight of the chopper falling, there is no sound. The absence of sound in my dream is scripted, as if there is intentionally no sound, but as soon as the ship disappears into the jungle, the noise, the sounds of chaos and panic, immediately return.

Bill Fuller, his eyes wide, fired the engines and throttled full forward, speeding toward the shore as boat captain Don Rogers grabbed the radio to report to headquarters. There was no noticeable panic in his voice. We were all experienced to the point that panic no longer fueled us. When something happened, even something as bad as a chopper going down, we were controlled enough to launch straight into data sharing communication, and Don was good at that.

His voice, filled with controlled urgency, reported the downing and gave coordinates. A short silence ensued on the other end, headquarters obviously absorbing the facts. During this silence, which lasted no more than three seconds as we were speeding toward the shore, I shouted to Don, "Ask permission for us to move in to check for survivors."

Anticipating approval, I began gathering grenades, my M16, and extra magazines, as did Billy and Richard Chaviers, a new kid from Chicago. Before the boat reached the shoreline, we had moved up on to the bow, ready to disembark and make our way through the jungle in the general direction of the downed chopper. Our intent was to recue anyone who'd survived the crash and/or recover weapons and equipment. The crux was, we had no idea what we were doing. All we had was intent and passion, and anyone in combat knows that "intent and passion," absent tactical skills and ability, are often all it takes to get you killed.

Permission came over the radio at about the same time the boat reached the shore. Fuller slowed only slightly, as the shoreline was thick with vines and tall bamboo shoots growing out of the muddy bottom. He had to plow through them with enough force to get us as close to solid footing as possible.

Don Rogers standing on the deck of a boat, the bank along the canal leading into and out of Sadec in the background.

As soon as the boat thudded to a stop, the edge of the bow still three or four feet from solid land, we jumped off into chest-deep water and mud and immediately began plowing forward through the growth.

In our rush to disembark and reach the chopper, and in our lack of infantry related skills, we neglected several things. Richard and I were still wearing sandals, none of us had thought to grab a radio for communications, and none of us had picked up a flak vest. From our vantage point in the river, it seemed as though the chopper had gone down mere yards from the shore. Though we hadn't time to discuss it, we were convinced we'd be off the boat no more than minutes before reaching the downed aircraft and crew. As we stepped in jelly-like mud, I took two strides before my sandals were immediately sucked off my feet.

Fuller throttled back and backed off the shore to better position the boat to provide support fire if necessary. We made it to relatively solid ground and began running, weapons ready, toward what we estimated to be the chopper's position. The jungle thickness allowed visibility of only a few yards ahead. My body was stressed to the point that I couldn't feel pain on my bare feet. I just kept running, as did Billy and Richard, each of us assuming the other two knew what they were doing, each of us unfortunately mistaken in that assumption.

As soon as our view of the river was obscured, we lost our only point of reference. With no directional capability, we succeeded in getting lost very quickly.

Fifty yards further into the jungle, we came to an almost circular clearing within which were a dozen bamboo-reinforced huts skirting the edge of the clearing. Fifteen or twenty of the inhabitants of this small village-like group were screaming and running chaotically in different directions, having seen the crashed chopper and heard our approach. We continued straight across the clearing in the direction we had set out from the boat.

In my dream, the chaos slows at this point to assure I have a clear view of what happened next, of the "right" I did. All the things I'd been told about such situations at that moment settled in on me and controlled my actions. I reacted. I didn't think. It was okay because we weren't supposed to think. We were supposed to react.

"If enemy fire comes from a specific location, all within that location are either enemy or enemy sympathizers," we were consistently instructed. This instruction must have been right because those who passed it along to us knew more than we did; they had the answers we didn't. They saw from a higher vantage point.

Suddenly from the corner of a hut structure, two men, a woman, and a child ran out in front of us. In my dream, the child is sometimes there and sometimes not. They continued running toward the edge of the clearing, screaming something unintelligible. We never slowed, and they, having jumped out in front of us, never slowed either until they reached the clearing's edge. There, just before us, they jumped into a hole in the ground. As I passed, seconds behind them, I instinctively pulled the pin from a grenade, dropped it into the hole, and continued out of the clearing and back into the jungle on the opposite side, still heading in the direction we assumed the chopper to be located. Seconds later we heard the explosion though we continued on, not looking back.

We kept running forward another five minutes or so until another chopper dropped down to about three feet off the ground, twenty yards in front of us. It hovered there in a small clearing, the door gunner frantically signaling us to get on board. As we jumped onto the chopper deck, the pilot lifted off and cleared the tops of the bamboo.

I was lying on my stomach, hanging on to a metal stanchion protruding out of the floor of the chopper as the craft rose swiftly into the air, my body from the waist down still hanging out over the edge of the deck. Billy and Richard had jumped on before me. They grabbed me by the shoulders and pulled me in.

Fully onboard, I turned and looked back at the jungle floor below us. The door gunner shook his head in disgust as he pointed. From our new vantage point in the air, we could clearly see 15–20 VC soldiers who had been closing in on our position below.

Our decision to try to locate the downed chopper had been a bad one. Armed with more intent and passion than knowledge, we had very nearly been overrun by a bunch of folks who knew what the hell they were doing. To make matters worse, from the time we cleared the thicket at the edge of the river, we had launched off in the wrong direction. If the chopper pilot hadn't dropped in to pick us up when he did, we'd have likely run straight into the enemy element.

The chopper was located the next day, the pilot and copilot still strapped in their seats. Weapons and communication equipment had been stripped. It was determined that a simple large caliber round had entered the gears on the main rotor and jammed them, causing the blade to slow to a stop. Several months would pass before the infection caused by the cuts on my bare feet began to heal. I didn't think about the grenade or who the people were who'd jumped into the hole in the ground for a few days after that. The regular reliving, the memories and the rationalizing, didn't begin for a few more weeks.

Since that day, I've chosen to believe things: that there was a hidden compartment directly under the ground and they escaped harm; or that there was no kid with them; or that the people who jumped into the hole had worked closely with the VC and maybe were even responsible for shooting the chopper down. I can occasionally fold these things into my dreams when they come to visit me at night.

Occasionally however, I can convince myself that it is okay. I can convince myself, that on that particular day, the thing I did was one of my "right" things.

26

A STRANGE MATURITY

Combat environments are amazing places for several reasons, but one of them is that they provide a "hands on" classroom in which the most vitally important of all life's lessons are taught and learned. A student in such a classroom can literally stand in one place, slowly rotate 360 degrees, and before he has returned to his original position, see a dead person (possibly for the first time), see a brutally slain dead person (almost certainly for the first time), have multiple near-death experiences himself, be wounded, and develop a clear, unambiguous understanding of what it means to be willing to sacrifice your very life so that another person, often one you don't even know, might live on. He can witness heroism and unfortunately, in rare cases, cowardice, and experience a multitude of other life-altering events that the average young man back in the normal world could never even imagine.

The Vietnam combat environment offered a little extra in this classroom. It offered a sort of massive chaos mixed in with these relatively common combat events. Vietnam threw in that confusion and chaos just to jazz things up a bit.

The students immersed in this learning environment were, in almost every sense, true students. Many had not even finished high school back home. Those who had graduated had often never lived by themselves; they'd simply lived at home with Mom and Dad one day, and set out for southeast Asia the next.

Few of them even knew how to get drunk in a sensible way, a way that didn't result in the dreaded "morning after." Many, especially those from the South, had never smelled the pungent aroma of marijuana, and virtually none of them had ever used opiates of any sort. Though the life-lessons we learned were intensified and solidified once we reached country, our actual emotional growth began back in the States, most often in and around our final debarkation points in California as we were preparing to leave for war.

26. A Strange Maturity

"Man, when I first went to California," I recalled one evening when we were drinking and taking part in a rare, honest, evaluation and comparison of our level of (dumb as a box of rocks) naiveté, "I was walking down the sidewalk in downtown Oakland one evening, most likely with my mouth hanging open. I was wearing civilian clothes, but I doubt anyone who happened to notice me was fooled by the disguise. I must have looked like a typical kid on a military pass. Anyhow, I spotted this Hells Angels guy getting off his bike and walking toward me on the sidewalk. He had typical motorcycle gang paraphernalia on his cutout, dungaree jacket, scraggly beard with an earring in one ear, and a damn pirate rag wrapped around his head. Had a look on his face like he'd be more than happy to kill anyone who stared at him for more than a second, but I just couldn't help it."

"I bet you looked like a 12-year-old hick from Mississippi," David laughed.

"You still look that way, David," Jack added. "Ain't that right, Uh-huh?"

"Uh-huhhhh," Billy added dutifully, drawing out the "huhhh" for emphasis.

"I know," I continued, "but I just couldn't help it. This guy had the coolest thing I ever saw in my life, and I just stared at him as he got close, and passed me by. He didn't even notice me. Like I wasn't even standing there."

"What was it?" they chimed in, leaning forward.

"He had a damn monkey on his shoulder; swear to God. A damn monkey on a chain, just sitting there on his shoulder; damn coolest thing I ever saw, until..." I paused at the perfect time.

"Until what, dammit," they implored.

I laughed and continued, following an appropriate pause for suspense, "Once he passed me by, I turned slowly and followed him with my gaze, still mesmerized. That damn monkey, unbeknownst to my new Hells Angels friend, had shit all down his back."

The laughter that followed subsided only after two or three of them had repeated, "Shit all down his back..." and "I'll be damned..." and "Wish to hell I coulda seen that."

For us, there was a perverse pleasure in taking part in these little episodes of self-disclosure. We felt comfortable in sharing, and it brought us closer as brothers.

Though few would admit it, many of the kids arrived at their debarkation points in California still virgins, still in love with their high school sweetheart, intent on a cottage and white picket fence when and if they got back home. Of those who were slightly more worldly, many had gained this

143

experience only weeks before their arrival, having had their first sexual experience in one of the military base towns in and around Los Angeles.

The girls of the evening who worked these areas learned several things early in the run-up to the war: (1) most of the guys who were being trained to fight in Vietnam were somewhat to extremely naïve; (2) Southerners, which almost guaranteed the former, would likely fall deeply in love with the first woman they slept with; (3) these guys were automatically enrolled in a $10,000 insurance policy; and (4) they likely had no one in particular in mind as a beneficiary.

The military went to great lengths to teach us all how to fight but spent little time or money teaching us how to avoid falling victim to the locals. As such, a thriving cottage industry was birthed, based on a simple con.

Many of these young prostitutes were very attractive. They had come to California hoping for a career in the movies, and were, therefore, good at playing such roles. Upon being solicited by a likely prospect, they'd refuse money on the first time out, convincing the mark that they couldn't help themselves. They had fallen in love and would never take money from *the man of their dreams.*

One thing would lead to another, and within a relatively short time, almost always end with the victim completely convinced that "love was true and never-ending," and that the object of their affection was the perfect beneficiary for their $10,000 insurance policy.

In later years some of these girls even reported some assistance, for a small fee, from the local administrators of the program. As soon as the kid had shipped out, the named beneficiary would contact the military insurance program and change her address, in the event the victim did what he was supposed to do and got killed. That way, they'd know where to mail the check. If he survived, on the other hand, and returned to the States, at which time the free policy would expire, his search for his true love would be fruitless since only the insurance policy processer knew the new address, and they wouldn't release it.

"Man," David commented, pointing at Billy and Jack and drawing out the "maaaannnn" in true "South-speak," indicating that one hell of a story was to follow. "Y'all remember that goofy-ass kid from Georgia? That, uhhh… Magee kid… Yeah that was his name … Otis Magee. Y'all remember him?" getting a non-committal nod of sorts from Jack and a grunt from Billy.

"He got engaged to one of those insurance hustler chicks in a bar outside Compton. She had talked the bartender into letting him in this sleazy hole that evening even though he was 19 or so, introduced him to the wonderful world of intimacy, and convinced him that she was in love before midnight. Hell, he came back to the base that morning, showing off a picture of the lovely thing and telling us how happy he was and how happy they were going to be when he got back from Vietnam. Damn kid wouldn't stop talking, and no one had the heart to tell him he'd been had."

David sighed slightly and continued, "Hell, he wouldn't admit it, but I guarantee you that was the first time that kid had ever gotten laid. Hell, he still had pimples. Kept looking in the mirror all morning, and I know damn well he was looking to see if he'd changed in any way or if any of the pimples were gone. He finally admitted he'd signed her on as his beneficiary as soon as the insurance office opened that morning."

"Yeah," Jack added. "Godfrey, you'd have to see him to know what we're talking about. That kid was Will Stockdale (referring to Andy Griffith's character in our beloved *No Time for Sergeants*) in the flesh."

"What'd she look like?" Jack asked.

"Ugly as pootin' in church," David replied, "but course everyone just sort of went on commenting on how she was the prettiest thing they'd seen since this and that and such. Didn't seem worth it to tell him the truth. We all figured it'd work out; he'd get over here and have a year to see things more clearly and go back to Georgia and marry Betty Sue or whoever, but…"

The mood changed in the tent, and everyone got quiet. The laugher slowly subsided the way it does when you recall something funny about the dearly departed at a funeral.

"But what…?" I prodded.

"Hell," Billy offered, "he wasn't ever gonna make it anyhow; we all knew that. I just never knew the part about the hooker."

"What?" I asked again.

"He died about a week after we got here," David said, then took a long pull from the bottle we were passing around.

"Didn't even have a chance to fire his weapon in an actual firefight," Jack said.

"How'd that happen?" I asked.

"Damn lucky he didn't kill anyone else," Jack continued. "Sittin' on the engine cover of one of the boats down in Vinh Long as they were driftin' in the river one day, playing around with a M79 grenade launcher. Damn kid fired a round straight up in the air, right above them. They never had time to fire the engines and get out from under it before it came straight back down on them. Luckily it hit the very edge of the railing right in front of him. All the blast force went right in his midsection, which is probably what kept anyone else from getting it."

Everyone sat quietly, just shaking their heads slowly. We took the opportunity to pass the bottle one more time.

"Guess the girl got the $10,000, huh," I said.

"Guess so," David added.

"Yep," Billy chimed in as David simply nodded.

"You know," I offered, following a seemingly appropriate silence, "I ain't that smart or anything, but I don't think I'd have fallen for something like that, or you Jack or Billy or any of us, for that matter. It just seems so obvious what she was doing. Course, none of those gals ever tried it with me."

"Maybe if it'd been a $50,000 policy," Jack added quietly.

The jab took a second to hit, but suddenly everyone erupted in laughter, with Billy and David throwing in a couple of "Hell, yeahs" and "Or maybe $100,000" for emphasis.

"Yeah, yeah," I acknowledged at length. "Nah, I'm just saying, I just don't think any of us would have fallen for it, is all."

"I don't think I would have either," Jack said, sinking back into reflective narrative, "but it ain't cause I'm smart or anything. It's just cause I've got someone back home, not a fiancée or anything, but just a 'someone,' you know."

"I think there's something about having that emotional connection back home," he continued, "something that sort of anchors you a little and kinda makes you feel that you're gonna make it over here because you're tied to something that probably won't cut you loose, you know."

"Maybe these guys, like Otis, were just looking for something to tie themselves to," he stumbled for the words, "not really thinking about it but sort of subconsciously. Maybe they just figured the same way; that if they had that connection, they'd be more likely to make it outa here and back home to something."

"Yeah," Billy added, "then all they'd have to do is learn not to fire a fucking grenade launcher straight up in the air, and they'd have it made."

"You know," David said. "One day we'll all just be ol' men sittin' around tellin' bored kids our stories. No one will listen to us; they'll just pretend to pay attention, but they won't listen. We'll be the ol' guy in the neighborhood screaming at kids to 'Get off my lawn!'" He waved his hands wildly.

David was the introspective one among us. He had a strange foresight which we all paid attention to unless he was predicting, as in this case, something we did not want to consider.

"If you mean, we're gonna be ol' farts," I offered, "that ain't likely. Actually, we probably won't make it out of here, and if we do, maybe being ol' farts will be a blessing from God. Besides, you're enough of an ol' fart right now to make up for the lot of us."

A perfect avenue out of the morose; we stifled a giggle, poured back a double shot each, and moved on to lighter things. As for poor ol' Otis, he was the one among us all that made the big mistakes, seemingly to teach the rest of us something. And though I never met him, he taught me a lesson I've tried hard over the years not to forget, and it had nothing to do with the direction in which I fired grenade launchers.

27

CLARITY OF VISION
RESERVED FOR ONE

For those who've never experienced it, it may come as a surprise that there is a very real, poetically spiritual, nature of tragedy in war. The beauty of life is stark and overwhelming in times of death and destruction. In its most tragic and unbelievably horrendous moments, war reveals to some the secrets of the universe. As such, these secrets can rarely be accepted out of that context.

Facing imminent and certain death, we hear things, we feel things, we experience things clearly, things that others can never accept. These things cannot and probably should not be explained.

Vietnam vets remember some things vividly. Others, they try to remember, but the recall is often clouded by hundreds of potential facts and emotions, and by other things you wish and hope were true. You wish and hope so hard at times until these things slip out of the category of wishes and hopes and desires, and land solidly into the cast of reality. They become like a movie you watch over and over again, willing the ending to be different. Only this movie runs in your subconscious so the ending can actually, occasionally be changed.

The vivid things remembered, however, never change. You see every detail, recall every smell and every sound. You can instantly retrieve even the pitch of the screams or duration of a solid string of unbroken automatic weapons fire, every fourth round a tracer, breaking the blackness of the night with an almost cheery, Christmas-like bright red or green, leaving behind trails of clarity like the trail behind a child's marker dragged across a blank sheet of paper.

One of those vivid things was the day Phil was at the front twin 50's, his left hand on the trigger, firing frantically, his right hand reaching out to shield and give comfort to the wounded girl lying on the deck next to him.

He was suddenly lifted from reality by a spiritual force so that he might look back into the gun tub below him, giving him a glimpse down into the Hell that awaited him. The very trajectory of a rocket fired directly at the bow of the boat reversed course in midflight, as if to accentuate the power of God over all mankind. There was the silent connection between a dying girl and the man leaning above her, trying to comfort her in her agony while still firing his weapon to keep them all alive.

Phil remembers that day. He remembers all the things a "Vietnam vivid" memory is supposed to leave with you. He remembers most clearly the things he doesn't want to remember. Like most of us, he's cursed with those memories.

"I just kept telling her, Godfrey, I knew she was scared and the sound of the fifties firing just above her head was hurting her; I just kept trying to tell her, 'It's gonna be okay. I have to keep firing or we'll all die here,'" Phil Yocum told me years later, his eyes fixed on a distant horizon as if he were still talking to her.

"So many things happened that day, and they were so real."

"She died later. Nothing I could do. We had injured folks everywhere when we backed off and headed out toward the river. She was just afraid, so I put her out in the open, up front by me so she could see better and where it would be cooler on the trip back to base. I tried to talk calmly to her even though she didn't understand what I was saying. Then when the shooting started, when we took the first rocket rounds, I just started shooting back, and she started screaming. Nothing I could do," he said, his head bowed slightly. "I tried to tell her, but there was nothing I could do."

"We were tired that morning. We'd been out all night, had a couple of skirmishes, you know, the kind that don't necessarily cause any damage, but just keep you all tied up inside like a tightly wound rubber band. We just wanted to get back and rest," Phil said.

He took a long deep breath, closed his eyes slightly and leaned back, staring at an imaginary movie screen on the ceiling, watching the events unfold once again.

"We got a call just as the sun was beginning to lighten the horizon with that dull shade of grey-green like it always did. You remember," he continued.

"Cougat called and directed us to that little outpost at Duc Ton. They'd been overrun that night, and there were wounded who needed to be picked up. Topping it off, a Special Forces colonel advisor was among them."

He looked back at me, shifted in his chair, and continued, "It was supposed to be a quick in and out, and of course, we didn't expect anything since the attack had happened only hours before. You remember, usually Charlie takes some time to regroup."

"When we got to the mouth of the canal, the tide was out, leaving no more than a foot of water at the entrance. We backed off and idled, waiting for the canal to fill up again so we could get in."

"Man, I remember waiting out there and just getting that spooky feeling that something was wrong. You remember what I'm talking about," he said, pointing a finger of emphasis in my direction.

"Anyhow, an hour or so passed, and we saw the canal had filled enough for us to get in. I was on the lead boat with Prendergast and Proffer. Prendergast was patrol lead that day, and he was as tired as the rest of us. Proffer was at the wheel."

"We headed into the canal at a pretty slow pace, since it was still a little shallow, and reached the outpost on the north side of the canal in fifteen minutes or so. As lead, our boat pulled in first and loaded the injured. They were waiting for us. We took on a dozen wounded plus the colonel. I had moved up on front guns and motioned them to lay the girl on the deck beside me. She had a nasty wound in her side, but she was still and quiet. You remember how the young folks there could take that pain and rarely whimper," he addressed me again.

As he did so, I recalled how Vietnam vets, when telling stories to other combat veterans, had a habit of pausing occasionally and making a connection with the listener by saying, "You remember," as if to reestablish their sanity by validating their recall.

"Anyhow," he continued, "the outpost had been attacked from the land side, and the Hueys had moved in before we got there, strafing the area pretty heavily. We moved quickly to clear the area, backing out and heading back west toward the main river. The canal had filled pretty well by then, but we still moved slow, being weighed down by all the extra folks onboard. Number two boat fell in behind us, fifty yards or so back. I remember as we rounded a curve and lost sight of 'two,' I heard a sort of muffled explosion from somewhere behind us."

"I looked at Prendergrast at the wheel to see if he had heard it. Before I had a chance to say anything, all hell broke loose." He paused, lost once again in the moment, likely absorbing the sights and sounds which came so clearly when recalling the vivid memories.

27. Clarity of Vision Reserved for One

"This blast and bright light jolted us upright out of the water a foot or so. I wheeled to the south side of the canal where the fire was coming from and opened up, the barrels of my fifties directly above the girl lying on the deck. I'll never forget how she was screaming and crying at the same time, holding her hands tight over her ears. I just kept pressure on the trigger bar with my left hand, moving the barrel direction across the ground level, and reaching out to grab her with my right. I knew she couldn't hear me, but I kept shouting, 'It's okay; it's okay!'"

"You know," he said, as a slight smile of recall creased his lips, "years later, when my son was a baby, he used to ride beside me in my truck when we'd go to the store or somewhere. If I had to put on the brakes suddenly, I'd always reach across in front of him, holding him back in the seat. Hell, I even do that now when someone's riding with me. From the very first time until now, when I reach across like that, that girl—I mean, her face, like she's still as young as she was then—appears before me. It's like it's her I'm holding back against the seat."

I wanted to say something like, "Yeah, I know what you mean," or "I understand that," or something, but I knew that being quiet and just listening was best. Anything I would have said at that time would have unfairly interjected "me" into his private recall. I would never have appreciated that if our roles were reversed.

He took a deep breath and continued. "The fire from the south bank just intensified. You remember how we could always slow the intensity of enemy fire when we opened up. That day, it was just the opposite. Seemed like our suppression fire just caused the faucet to open; I mean rockets, AK rounds, the works, just kept pouring in."

"I looked toward Proffer to see why he wasn't throttling full forward to get us out of there and saw the colonel behind the wheel."

"You know how strange thoughts come to you at times like that," he smiled. "Damnedest thing. I remember thinking, hell, he don't know how to drive the boat. He needs to get out of the way and turn the wheel back over to Proffer."

"Suddenly another rocket slammed into the side of the boat, shifting us toward starboard and knocking me most of the way out of the gun tub. I realized the boat was still moving, and the colonel had been thrown away from the wheel. We had just slipped around another curve in the canal, partially out of the field of fire. I jumped down behind the wheel to keep us moving away from the attack as much as possible. That's when I saw Proffer."

He paused and took another deep breath. In the silence, I felt guilt at my question.

"Proffer...," he stopped short, and I knew a vision that had haunted him most of his life had been recalled from the depths of his memory yet again, and I knew it was because I'd asked him to relive that day.

I opened my mouth to apologize when he interrupted me and continued. "Proffer was lying face down, beside the engine cover. Half his head was gone, and what was left just didn't look human."

Dead silence ensued. I wasn't willing to break it, and Phil just sat there thinking and staring at the floor, his face totally expressionless as if Proffer was lying before him once again. He wasn't crying or showing any signs of emotion like quivering lips, the precursor to tears. He was just recalling the moment matter-of-factly, like he was testifying in court. Combat veterans learn over time how to recall events like that, completely emotionless. It may be because they do it so many times, or it may just be an emotional shield our subconscious develops. The problem with it is that at those times when we need to express honest emotion, such as the death of a loved one much later in life, we have trouble regaining that tug of appropriate sorrow.

"You know," he began at length, "if that had been any other circumstance or any other day in any other location in the world, I've often wondered if I would have cried out, or cursed, you know the way you do when something shocks or surprises you. As it was, I just looked at him a second; seemed longer but I'm sure it was only a second, sort of like I thought maybe he was supposed to look like that."

"Anyhow," he continued following another pause, "the colonel was down beside Proffer, but he was still moving a little. I looked back toward the rear mount, toward Lake, standing at the fifty. It sort of seemed like he was holding it really tight, like he was afraid of losing it or something, but he wasn't firing. I started to say something to him, but that's when I noticed his entire midsection was gone, like someone had opened him up to see what was inside him. He was dead; just standing there, dead."

"I guess about that time I realized that I too had been hit. Musta happened when we took the last rocket. I didn't really feel much, you know. I'd reached out to help the colonel get to his feet when I realized that my arm wouldn't work. It just hung there like it belonged to someone else and just had no intention of responding to my attempt to use it. It was kinda surreal, actually. The idea that there was so much blood, and I could see inside the arm and could see muscle tissue and bone and stuff, and I didn't feel any-

Remains of one of the boats in the firefight where Phil Yocum was wounded.

thing; hell, that scared me most. I mean, you're supposed to feel pain when something like that happens, and it's just not natural not to."

He continued, this time looking at me and using his hands to gesture, emphasizing his comments instructively. I felt easier seeing him in a less contemplative state, more conversing. "Luckily, I heard a shout from the bank. By this time, we were out of firing lanes, and the shooting had stopped for a minute. I felt like the 'Bells of St. Mary' were going off in my head, but I did see the soldier on shore waving us over. As soon as I grabbed the wheel and turned in that direction, we beached in the mud. I kept the engines in low power so we'd stick there. I thought I was seeing things, man, but there were two Huey gunships on the ground just behind this guy, almost as if by magic."

He pointed his finger at me and continued in a slow, methodically in-structive tone as if to say, "Don't forget this, Godfrey. It means something."

"One of the Huey pilots told me later at the hospital that he had gotten a radio call ordering him to go to that location, land, and wait for instructions."

"Damn it, Godfrey, that pilot never found out who had called him, and there were no records of anyone directing him to do that." He continued leaning forward in his chair. "He never found out where the orders came

153

from. He was just told to head there and land at that location. That means something, man. It means something."

"Once off the boat," he said, "I just dropped on my back there in the mud on the canal bank. I closed my eyes off and on for the next few minutes as the wounded and the dead were brought off the deck. I remember seeing the girl being carried off by one of the soldiers, her head and arms dangling. Her eyes were open and staring in my direction as she was carried past me. She looked at me as if she was saying that she wasn't mad, you know, as if she knew that I had tried to help her, as if she knew I didn't want her to hurt like that."

"Oh, Lord," he continued, like he had lifted a great burden and carried it a ways and finally gotten a chance to lay it down. "On the chopper flight back in to the field hospital, Prendergast died. I never figured out exactly what killed him cause he wasn't shot up like the rest of them. His head was in my lap, and he just went to sleep. He'd been moaning and gasping, and I guess he had some bad internal injuries, and suddenly he just closed his eyes and drifted off. I remember thinking that I was supposed to be feeling something, you know, fear or remorse or sadness or anger, but it was almost like I'd just gone out and run some errands or gone to the store or something, and I was on the way back home. I didn't feel anything, like all the things that had happened were supposed to happen. And then, I closed my eyes and went to sleep, just like Proffer, fully expecting to wake up in Heaven. Next thing I knew, I was in the hospital, folks scrambling all around me. That's when I found out that me and one other kid I'd never even talked to that much... You know how hard it was to talk to the new kids; how we always used to avoid that; same way the ol' guys use to avoid us when we first got to country, I suppose. Anyhow, we were the only two to survive on the lead boat ... me and that kid... What was his name?" he concluded introspectively.

He was more matter-of-fact now. "I saw the kid before he was shipped out. He wanted to tell me thanks for saving his life. 'Thanks for saving his life...' Makes me proud when I think back on that even though I don't know what I did that made him feel like I'd saved his life."

"Never have spoken to him since then. He was shipped back to the States next day. Maybe I'll try to find him one day," he said softly. "Maybe ... maybe not. I don't know."

28

Always Begin with "You Ain't Gonna Believe This Shit"

Anyone who experienced combat in Vietnam, for any length of time, can tell of things that happened that shouldn't have, not because they were wrong or morally unjust or that they were mistakes. They simply shouldn't have happened because they defied all logic, like things that fell up instead of down.

In most cases, these things happened during firefights, when by all rights you should be dead, yet there you were, telling the story instead of lying in a queue on a Tan Son Nhut airstrip in a black vinyl bag, waiting to be loaded on a homebound aircraft. Some of these things, in retrospect, can be easily explained, but for those involved—those closest to the events—they are nothing short of miracles, mythical and deity driven. A man's miracle is sacred to him.

To better understand these events, not necessarily the tangible elements, but the fact that they occurred or were believed to have occurred at all, one must understand that in Vietnam—the Vietnam that we knew in 1968—there were no rules. Things that controlled natural occurrences in any other part of the world just didn't function in Vietnam. Laws such as that of Newton, as well as other laws of physics and laws of nature, in that place, at that time, were totally suspended.

In the early spring of '68, a few weeks after Tet, the men of 513 were still on a fairly high alert status. The fact that the NVA and VC, all Ho's boys, were serious about the war had been amplified by the offensive itself. This knowledge, coupled with the fact that our individual chances of surviving had decreased correspondingly, was definitely not lost on us.

We were more cautious when we checked the ubiquitous sampan or small junk for contraband. We watched the eyes and hand movements of the "indigs" (indigenous people), even those we thought we knew well. We kept our guard up higher and for longer periods of time, and unless necessary, we stayed out of the smaller, narrower canals. The problem with this, however, was that we were called to missions in the smaller canals with much more frequency than before Tet.

PBRs were at a great disadvantage in canals. The muddy, ditch-like waterways were shallower and of course narrower, reducing our capability for speed and maneuverability. Billy and David referred to them as creeks and joked about having an almost uncontrollable urge to strip off and go swimming in them every time we entered one.

"Kinda makes you homesick, don't it, 'Uh huhhhh?" David would prompt Billy.

"Uh huhhhh," Billy would respond, inexplicably hanging a deep Southern drawl on the retort.

Humor aside, the canals definitely put us at a disadvantage, and though we joked about it now and then, no one let their guard down. In most of these slight tributaries, a B40 rocket fired from either bank had no more than a dozen yards or so to travel before impact. We were the proverbial sitting ducks.

On the open river, we could always get out of range of just about any type of weapon, but of course we weren't very effective out there. We had to be "up close and personal" if we were going to do our job. Our job wasn't to get out of range. Our job wasn't to be safe. Strangely enough, we wouldn't have had it any other way. The canals and winding tributaries, wrapping and snaking their way through the dense jungles, were where glory waited. They beckoned, and we found our manhood there.

Still, we didn't call ahead. Spontaneous canal checks were safer for obvious reasons. The VC didn't generally set an ambush in random locations on the offhand chance that a patrol might come by. We were much more cautious, however, when we'd been directed to those areas or were there in the aftermath of some type of firefight or attack on an outpost. These types of missions and orders were on the uptick in the weeks following Tet.

Doyle Hensley, a 20-something, good-looking kid from Ohio, had been promoted to boat captain much faster than the rest of us because he was sharp and observant and had a leadership quality that usually had to be learned slowly over a long period of time. Once he took over his own boat, everyone wanted to work with him for all the obvious reasons. As boat captain, he could have avoided the most hazardous of tasks, assigning them to

Surprise canal patrol. Canals were the most dangerous place for PBRs to operate for obvious reasons, but occasional checks for enemy activity were required. Strangely, these patrols were sought after by PBR crews since, as one seasoned crew member put it, "If you're gonna go swimming, you gotta get wet."

one or more of his crew, but Doyle wouldn't do that. He was always first in line when something "hairy" was on tap and seemed almost fearless. On this day, for this mission, he had taken the forward fifty position, having his gunner operate the boat.

The patrol had been sent up a canal off the Co Chien river, one of the three branches of the Mekong that split off just south of Vinh Long and rambled southward toward the sea. A Vietnamese army outpost had been hit the night before and several casualties needed evacuation. The attack was eerily similar to other enemy operations along the rivers in the weeks following Tet, and Charlie knew someone would be sent there.

"Man, I just had this weird feeling, you know," Doyle recalled in conversation over beers at the compound's make-shift beer joint a couple of nights after the event.

"This hadn't been long after Proffer and Lake and those guys got shot up so bad, and Yocum damn near lost an arm, remember. Hell, it was the same damn setup too; outpost gets shot up, casualties needed evac, and you know damn well Charlie knows who's gonna be sent in to get 'em out. Perfect fit for an ambush." He pointed a slender, instructive finger in our direction, waving it slowly from one to another, assuring agreement among us all.

A common practice, especially in the aftermath of Tet, was the use of PBRs to make WIA and KIA extractions along the rivers and canals rather than risk a Huey MEDEVAC. Additionally, the helo crews were in constant demand further inland, and U.S. military personnel wounded in combat were normally prioritized in their missions. It took longer, but was a natural fit for PBRs to conduct such extractions. Charlie had grown wise to this process and had learned to take advantage of it.

"I just had a strange feeling, so I took the forward gun and had Graham take the wheel."

The two-boat patrol conducted a textbook extraction, with Doyle's lead boat sitting slightly offshore to provide cover while the follow-on boat beached and took on the wounded. The canal, approximately a klick or two in length and 200 yards wide, was horseshoe in shape, exiting off the river at one point and winding around back into the Co Chien further downriver.

"The plan, since the outpost was only a couple of hundred yards in, was to pick up the wounded and make a quick 180 back to the main river and home. We radioed ahead and told them to have everyone prepped and waiting on the canal bank. Then we slipped off the main river about 1000 hours, heading for them. As we cruised in, the place was like a ghost jungle."

He looked quizzically, squinting his eyes and waving his open hand slightly, for effect. "You know how the kids kinda gather along the bank when boats are passing? Hell, you can even spot birds or damn monkeys jumping around or something. None of that. Nothing. Place was just dead all the way in."

After action reviews determined that the VC had set the ambush perfectly. They hit the outpost the night before and appeared to clear the area. In actuality, they'd quietly set up heavy machine guns and multiple B40s on both sides of the river with their directing fire facing inward from the river. The strategy was to prevent the boats from turning around and exiting back toward the main river once they'd engaged. It was similar to the way fish traps are made, allowing the prey to swim in but preventing an exit out the same way, in effect driving them further into the canal where reinforcements were set up on both sides. The boats would be caught in a crossfire that would be relentless as they sped deeper inland to escape the onslaught.

"You know how a typical firefight will involve an initial hail of shit, then slow for a minute or so before it picks back up?" he said.

I caught myself nodding, as did the others around the table since we all actually *did* know exactly what he was talking about.

"This one didn't. Man, once they opened up, the air was filled with metal for what seemed like an hour."

"Shit," Billy offered in support.

"For some reason, they did wait for the follow-on boat to load the WIAs and back off from the beach a little."

"Wanted to slow your ass down," David prompted, as Billy and Jack offered a confirming, all-knowing, "Hell yeah" and "Fucking A, man."

"Well, they did that," Doyle continued, "and the only clear path we had was straight into the canal; way too hot to try and turn around, and at the time it didn't seem that there was anything coming from deeper in."

He took a swig of beer, wiped his face, and caught his breath before continuing. "We had to slow to allow the follow-on boat to keep up with us, but no sooner had we headed into the jungle than all hell broke loose in front of us. Shit flyin' everywhere. Man, I just kept the key down on those front guns, wiping them across one side of the bank for a second, then shifting to the other side, then back to the first side. Just everything I could do to slow the intensity of fire. The air was so full of shrapnel and bullets that there was no place to duck or dodge. I had to keep my attention on the spot I was shooting and hope none of the bullets decided to choose that exact same pathway."

All firefights seem to last for hours, just like when you leave your finger on a hot stove once you've touched it. In reality, they were short-lived, since, unless we were immobilized, we could eventually clear the area. The patrol that day did escape the fire corridor, miraculously intact. They'd pushed further into the canal at as high a rate as they could with the extra weight of the evacs, eventually arriving back on the main river through the other end of the horseshoe. To be safe, they continued to the opposite side of the river, calling for air MEDEVAC to meet them on shore.

"You know, when we first started drawing fire," Doyle continued, "you ain't gonna believe this shit, but in the confusion, I didn't even realize it till later, but...."

As he paused and shook his head, sharing a moment of disbelief with himself, David threw up his hands and interjected, "Believe what, man? Damn. Go on!"

"When the shooting first started, I saw a trail stream from a B40 heading straight toward the bow of the boat like it was gonna impact just below the waterline. I sort of subconsciously assumed I'd be dead in a second. The boat, I remember, shuddered a little, and I heard a loud explosion on the opposite bank, but with all the activity, I just kept firing. Pretty soon, I guess it just slipped my mind with everything going on. We got to the other side of the river and beached the boats pretty far up on the sand bank. Damn tide went out by the time the choppers got there and took the WIAs away, and hell, we were high and dry. No way we could get back onto the waterway and out of there any time soon. We just pushed together on the hull till we righted the boats and propped them, waiting for the tide to come back in.

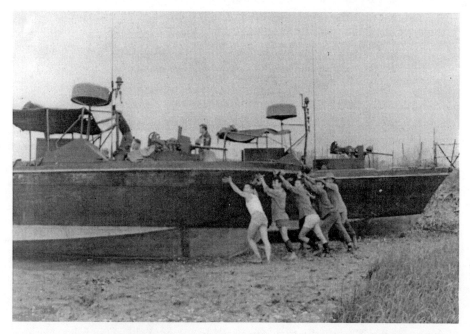

Doyle Hensley's boat, grounded in low tide, shortly after this firefight. The hole in the hull is slightly visible near the left hand of the man second from left. None of the crew members are identifiable in this photograph.

A later shot of Doyle Hensley (right) and Bill Fuller standing by Seawolf gunship.

Luckily it was a secure area, but just in case, we called in a Seawolf patrol to hang out till we could get the boats back in the water."

"When we finally got a look at the hull to check for damage, there was a hole." He paused for emphasis, holding his hands up forming a ten-inch hole. "A damn hole was there, in one side and out the other."

"Right below my guns," he added slowly for appropriate emphasis. "Right below my nuts, as a matter of fact."

That was Doyle Hensley's miracle.

"Son of a bitch," Jack offered, slowly accentuating each word, as David and Billy instinctively looked down at their own genitals, and I subconsciously cupped my hands around mine.

29

COUNTERINSURGENCY: TWO BEAUX WOOING THE SAME GIRL

The Vietnam conflict was a counterinsurgency operation. In fact, it was the epitome of counterinsurgency operations, and it ramped up at a time when the conventional United States military had little sophisticated knowledge of such operations in terms of how to execute. Many at command levels across the nation likely didn't even know how to spell it.

The fact that America would be called upon for coming generations to conduct such operations was understood and known by only a few military strategists, primarily as a result of Cuba. But the actual doctrine, the counterinsurgency doctrine, was not defined and adapted to the military playbooks at the command level until well into the mid–60s.

In effect, we were attempting to do something that was extremely complex, something we really didn't even know we could do, and something we definitely didn't know exactly how to do. The worst part of it, however, was that the heavy lifting, the actual implementation of counterinsurgency operations, was delegated to guys like me and Jack and Billy and David, and Phil Yocum and Bill Fuller and Don Rogers and our command element, at a time when we could still vividly remember flunking out of Mrs. Doreen Alexander's 10th grade history class. It was like taking a bunch of well-meaning, but naïve high school dropouts and assigning them the task of designing and implementing a complex social program, a program which would determine the outcome of the Vietnam War.

While it is true that Special Forces teams had been conducting Foreign Internal Defense (FID) missions throughout the world for some time, missions that entailed dropping into locations populated by indigenous groups and making necessary connections, the somewhat related, albeit much more complex, counterinsurgency doctrine was still not clearly understood.

29. Counterinsurgency

Special Forces had been doing similar operations in Vietnam for a couple of years before large numbers of conventional troops were sent in. Special Forces operations, however, were to be followed by a cadre of conventional forces, commanded mostly by senior noncommissioned officers (NCOs) and officers, all steeped in conventional warfare backgrounds from Korea and World War II. These folks at tactical command levels were unfamiliar with the technicalities and nuances of counterinsurgency operations. Even today, "counterinsurgency" is rife with nuances and inconsistencies, and the most intelligent strategists argue about every aspect of it, including the best way to do it.

Counterinsurgency is a type of warfare that is conducted in order to defeat insurgents who are intent on successful insurgency operations. An insurgency, conducted by individuals referred to as insurgents, has an objective of convincing a populace to support them in their ultimate goal, a goal of fundamentally changing an existing government or possibly destroying it all together and implementing a completely different one. The counterinsurgency effort is designed to thwart this goal. And at the center of this push/push-back are ordinary people intent on nothing more than survival and putting food on the table.

In effect, the process can be seen as two beaux courting the same girl. Of course, the prize is much more complex and has international implications, but the process, in a sense, is just that simple.

As is the case in many such competing social occurrences, occasionally one of the "beaux" will adopt and implement the "Me or Nobody" policy: *I'll woo you and shower you with goodies, but if you don't agree and come with me, I'll kill you.* Let's call that beau the North Vietnamese.

The other beau, in this case America and its allies in Vietnam, in order to win the affection of the prize, implemented a policy that is still today discussed and undertaken in nations around the world: "Winning the Hearts and Minds." While America's efforts in Vietnam were more altruistic, we were, in fact, just as serious about winning. The basic idea is fairly simple; if the chick prefers you to the other guy, she will send him packing on her own.

Again, on the ground implementation of this complex endeavor, an endeavor that wasn't fully understood and doctrinally implemented until the mid–60s (many argue that it is still not fully understood even today), fell to us. We were charged with winning the hearts and minds. We were charged with winning the affection of the girl in the middle, thereby thwarting the efforts of "Ho's boys," the VC and NVA.

Brothers in the Mekong Delta

The greatest obstacle we faced, however, was the fact that we were charged with turning her head away from a suitor who was as close as her brother, her neighbor, her former best friend; he was a suitor who spoke her language and understood the extremely complex values of her father and her grandfather. And we had no idea how to do it, or even a cursory understanding of what it was, or for that matter, the fact that we were even doing it.

In the early days of the war, we enjoyed the "honeymoon" period. Americans and American soldiers are seen by the average populace of less economically successful countries as rich people who carry wondrous things in their pockets to hand out to the children. They're seen as strange people from strange lands who can, without a second thought, produce brand new, shiny soccer balls or shoes that keep out the water and don't have holes in them. They are seen as people who are anxious to hand these things out to anyone with an outstretched hand.

In Vietnam, in the beginning, we truly were "GI number one." We held on to that status as long as possible and in many areas of the interior, far away from the bustle of Saigon. In the back country where we were rarely encountered by the local farmers and their families, we maintained that aura for years.

By the time Jack and Billy and David and a little later, I, got there, however, the luster had faded. We still had the wondrous things in our pockets, and we could still come up with a new soccer ball at a moment's notice, but the people began to see that we were just as flawed, if not more so, than everyone else. Some of us were downright assholes. Regardless, we were still charged with wooing the girl and winning the hearts and minds. The guys of 513 took that charge to heart. As a matter of fact, we enjoyed the task.

"These people are just like us," Billy would often say, "or if you prefer, we're just like them. We're all as good and as bad as we would be back home and as they are on a daily basis."

There was some comfort in knowing that. It sort of took the edge off, because we knew how to be good folks back home, and we knew how to be assholes back home. We were just functioning as normal, only on a different stage. Of course, we didn't call it counterinsurgency operations. By the same token, we didn't call it "winning the hearts and minds" either. That was the clever line of some politician in D.C., and we laughed at it. We just called it being a decent human being. We screwed it up at times, but no more than we'd screwed it up back home.

29. Counterinsurgency

The fact is, and the thing people often lose sight of is, that we wanted to do things that helped. Actually, in most cases, human nature drives us in that direction. It's not purely an altruistic instinct either. People feel a sense of empowerment when they do things that alter another's attitude or sense of wellbeing.

In Vietnam, we could buy a couple of packs of cigarettes from a street vendor kid and tip him a dollar, and he'd go home with as much as he made in the entire week before. We knew the effect of our relatively simple, benign gesture. It made us feel at times like we had superpowers. With the simple gesture of a dollar tip, we could alter an individual's entire day. There was, as such, a bit of a selfish component to it, but the ends were met. At least they were most of the time.

Fishermen in Vietnam never discarded catch because it was too small or not the exact type of fish they were looking for. They kept and consumed absolutely everything they pulled from the river. Small fish the size of minnows would be mixed whole into boiling rice and consumed.

When a couple of fishermen in their flimsy cutout sampans would pole alongside us during the day, it empowered us and gave us a sense of pride to see the looks on their faces when we tossed a grenade over the side, allowed it to sink a few feet then explode, stunning and sending to the surface a bevy of fish of all sorts, small to large. The fishermen would shout "toi oi" (loose translation: "son of a bitch, look at that") and scurry around to gather the fish before they recovered and swam away.

When we went to Vietnam, we were boys who were in the process of becoming young men. We went with the desire to do good, to be good. We didn't, contrary to the belief of some at the time, go there to be killers or to "defeat" an enemy.

Though some may have hidden this fact, hoping to present to their contemporaries a much more callous, war-fighter persona, I was fortunate. I had friends like Jack and Billy and David and the rest of the guys. They all emphasized the former persona: the "good guy." It was simple, really. They, themselves, were just good kids and as such, respected the true goodness in others.

In Vietnam, there was another side to this coin. Human beings often do good for those less fortunate because it makes them feel powerful and "cleansed" in a way, as if their "good" wiped out their "bad." Subconsciously, they expect a modicum of appreciation and acknowledgment.

The excitement in the eyes or smile on the face of a kid who's just received a new soccer ball or a new pair of shoes is acknowledgment enough for most. The pleasant nod of the head from a man who is given a lift instead of having to walk or is allowed to scoop up a full day's fish in a few minutes is enough.

In the depths of our boyish hearts, we wanted to be appreciated for risking death on Vietnamese soil. We wanted the people we were there to liberate or protect from harm to acknowledge the sacrifice of ourselves and our brothers. When we didn't see that, or when we saw the opposite, when we saw the resentment, we often did not have the maturity to understand it. And to be blunt and simplistic, it sort of hurt our feelings.

Jack understood it and Billy understood it and David understood it. I wanted to understand it, mostly because I felt inadequate in their presence at not being able to understand it, but the fact is, from time to time, it pissed me off.

"Don't they understand what the hell we're trying to do here?" I'd complain occasionally over beers or swigs of JD in the tent.

"What are we trying to do here?" Billy or Jack would reply, knowing full well that I'd have no canned comeback.

"Fuck, you know," I'd reply haltingly, the laughter at my mumbling already building to a crescendo. "I don't know, hell, win some hearts and minds or some shit. I don't know."

As the laughter would subside, David would once again state the obvious, the obvious that my irritation had not allowed me to see, *once again*. "Man, these people ain't dumb. They know we're just a part of something that's been going on here since before they were born and will be going on probably until they die, and they're smart enough to understand that you're just doing it for a year or two, and you're going home."

"Hard on all of us to lose guys like Musetti and Graham and all of them, but these folks have been losing mamas and daddies and brothers and such for generations, and they probably don't understand why either."

"Yeah," Jack replied, "and the fact of the matter is we—you and me and David and Billy—ain't getting anything out of being here. We're sacrificing everything just like we're trained to do, but there are a whole bunch of fat cats in D.C. who're getting a hell of a lot out of us being here, have a hell of a lot riding on us being here, and these folks, though they may look like they're disconnected from all that, these folks know that."

A few years had passed, and the honeymoon was over between the Vietnamese people and American servicemen. We had become simply people, people from different cultures and different nations, but people nonetheless, and familiarity had truly begun to breed contempt.

There was bad to that, but there was also *good*. People began to see beyond nationality and recognize human nature and character, or the lack thereof. Friendships began to develop, and people even began to fall in love.

We resented each other at times, and at times embraced those we admired and wanted to be associated with, but it was all based on the same criteria that we and the Vietnamese people used with members of our own culture. And in the process, occasionally really great things happened, things that the media didn't laud, because in most cases there was little blood and violence associated.

Often these "great things" were small and insignificant, but had truly impactful, long lasting effects; the old Vietnamese who stopped a soldier from walking down a worn path because he knew there were mines planted there; the young woman who wiped a wounded soldier's head with a cool cloth to offer a simple reprieve from pain; the American soldier who helped an elderly woman shoulder a burden she was carrying for a short while; a million simple interactions, every day, transcended cultures and nationalities and reflected, simply, human beings interacting.

These things would be remembered forever and reflected upon from time to time throughout the lives of those who witnessed or took part in them. And now and then, one of these "great things" would rise from the simple to the heights and would be etched above all other things in our minds.

"You should have been there," Don Rogers said. "I'll never forget it. I had no idea what I was doing, really."

That day, Don and Phil Yocum had been part of a patrol conducting routine river traffic checks. The post–Tet skirmishes were still impacting us all, but they had begun to slow, allowing us to get back to somewhat of a pre–Tet routine. Though we were always waiting "for the other shoe to drop," we all welcomed the lull in activity.

"They just came alongside without being hailed," I added. Usually people on the river were too busy to volunteer for searches and had to be called over.

"Hell, they didn't just 'come over,'" Don responded. "They were hell bent to get alongside. So much we all grabbed our weapons expecting an attack or a grenade tossed at us. Once they came around that sharp curve, you know, up by that ferry crossing north of the canal and spotted us, man, they veered sharp, right towards us and kicked it into high gear. Thought we was goners."

Phil was a lot like Billy, always the calm voice among us. As Don slowed to take another swig of beer, Phil took over the narrative. His voice this time, however, betrayed the "calmness." But it was more of an excitement that might come from a child telling his buddies what he got for Christmas instead of the usual excited tone elicited by having narrowly escaped shrapnel from a rocket attack.

"Didn't take long for us to realize they just needed something, and probably weren't going to throw a frag at us. As they approached, they were hollering something and waving that hand up and down, you know like they do when they want you to stop. The terp said they needed something, but even he couldn't understand what, cause they were all screaming at the same time. We could see two older guys and one younger, and they kept pointing to something on the boat."

"Man, I don't know," Jack offered, at a slack point in the narrative. "Not sure I coulda held back. I would have probably popped a round toward them anyhow."

"Yeah, I know what you mean, but there was something about Cowboy's response to them."

Cowboy was one of the most popular interpreters in the section and happened to be on the same boat as Phil and Don that day.

"Cowboy didn't seem to be gearing up for a fight, and you know he usually spots these sneak actions pretty well. He just shook his head a little confused and held his hand up in a way that eased the tensions a bit."

Don jumped back into the narrative, leaning forward to reclaim the conversation. After all, it was his story more than anyone else's.

"When they got closer, we could clearly see someone laying on the deck of the boat: a young woman, holding her stomach and moaning. I thought for sure she'd been shot or something, but I didn't see any blood anywhere."

"About that time, Cowboy got all excited and started shouting, 'She have baby. She have baby!'"

"It was really kinda funny," he giggled. "You know how we all react to being attacked. You know, when a rocket drops in a few feet from us, and the damn shit hits the fan all of a sudden. I never see any of you guys ever even shout anything. You all just move into position and grab your shit and start returning fire. We do it every time, like we woke up that morning doing it, like it's nothing more than a routine interruption in the day."

"Cowboy," everyone's favorite interpreter.

He laughed at this point, and even the ever-calm Phil joined with a noticeable giggle. "Man, you'd a thought we were getting into our first ever firefight. Hell, we all started running around, going nowhere and bumping into each other. I laughed my ass off later. Even ol' grizzly beard yelled, 'Get some hot water!' Shit, we all broke up, still running back and forth while their boat tied off."

"Even Cowboy was freaking out. He just kept jumping around and shouting, 'She have baby. She have baby.' Funny as hell."

"I just kept thinking," Don said. "Man, the shooting and the rockets and frag grenades and shit is one thing. That's what we all came for, but birthing babies, well hell, I just didn't expect that."

"But," a pause ensued while Don formulated the conclusion of the narrative, "I looked at Phil, and he looked at me, and swear to God, we didn't say a word. We just jumped down on the sampan deck, and everybody stopped running around and stopped shouting and just looked at us. It was weird as hell. One minute it was total chaos, and you couldn't hear a thing for all the shouting and shit, and the next," he snapped his fingers, "quiet enough to hear a rat pissin' on cotton."

"Phil knelt down by the lady's head and cradled her head on his lap, talking real calm like, and I put my hands on her stomach, real gentle like, so as not to scare her or anything. She stopped screaming and such and just sort of started moaning, and there was no doubt she was in a lot of pain."

"Yeah," Phil chimed in, a smile on his face, his voice calm. "It was just sort of natural, you know. Don had lived on a farm when he was a kid, and we just sort of both knew that he was the best to handle the birth since he'd most likely seen it a lot. Hell, I'd never even seen an animal give birth, but I did know how to calm her a little. I just held her head in my lap and talked real quietly, and the slower and the quieter I got, the quieter and calmer she got. Man, it was the neatest thing I ever did and ever will do; there's not a doubt in my mind."

Don held his finger up in the air, cocked his head, and squinted one eye ever so slightly as a college professor making an important point. "I knew one thing about births; I knew a baby has to come out head first, and just laying my hands on her stomach, I don't know how I could tell, but I just knew that baby was feet first, trying to come out. She had an ol' stinky blanket across her waist, and I just pulled it aside."

"There was something really beautiful about her right then, you know," Don said much more quietly, as if he were trying to remember exactly what she looked like. "I mean laying there totally naked from the waist down. It wasn't sexy or like looking at a woman with no clothes or anything like that. She just looked beautiful, you know, almost noble or majestic or something."

"Okay, so you didn't feel a rush," David said, rolling his hand over in a circle, encouraging him to go on. "So, what the hell happened, man?"

"Okay, okay," Don jumped back into the narrative. "Don't ask me how cause I can't explain it. Guess it must have been God guiding my hand or something, but I could feel the baby's little feet kicking around and stuff, right down there in the lower part of her stomach, and I knew that wasn't right, so I just started massaging the little thing real gently."

"Yeah," Phil chimed in, "it was neat. He was talking to the little feller real gentle like, you know, 'Okay, slow down now, you're gonna be fine but you gotta do this the right way.' Hell, I almost cried."

"All of a sudden," Don said, haltingly the way a magician will do when unveiling the conclusion of a trick, "he just rotated around, and suddenly his head popped out, really slow at first. Then it just slipped out like a balloon you squeezed till it slides out the other side of your hand. Then, hell, there he was, all wet and slimy and yelling like a typical pissed off baby."

In that moment, the moment that baby came into the world, they were just people—not American or Vietnamese people—but just people. And in that moment, they came together and did what had to be done to make sure that beautiful little baby boy joined us all in our adventure here in life. That was one of those moments when "really great things happened."

The following week, that mother and her husband and father and father-in-law all came to the post and presented to Don and Phil and all of us the young, smiling, and healthy "PBR Nguyen Quang."

30

SO, WHAT DO
WE DO NOW?

When we left Vietnam, we needed each other. Though we didn't realize it at the time, all Vietnam veterans upon coming home needed each other. We needed each other because we were different. Like veterans of every war in history, we all came home as someone other than the person we were when we left. We were the tunnel rat who was trapped when a tunnel collapsed on him and now has to sleep outside most of the time because of overwhelming claustrophobia. We were the POW who was tortured by having his hand mangled in a meat grinder and today has to be restrained from slamming his hand against walls because he is driven to recreate that pain. Like Jack, who left as a fun-loving kid from his community—a kid everyone wanted to be around—and came back a young man who sought out confrontation, getting into multiple fistfights in his first few years back home. Some of us came home with an intense fear of darkness or an abhorrence of certain smells or sounds because they were associated with the death we had seen in country. We matured, like most kids around the world, but our maturity was infected with a strange gene of some sort. Something was wrong with us, and we had no idea what. And because we came home hated by a large portion of the nation, we wouldn't talk about it. Some of us even came home feeling that everyone who spit on us was right and that we deserved any pain we had to endure. As is the case with anyone who experiences pain or discomfort, we thought we were the only people in the world who felt that way. The isolation made it worse. Even those who loved us simply wanted us to "get over it." When we left Vietnam, we needed each other. But because we were hated in those early years, we shunned each other. We shunned the very people who could assure us that we weren't freaks, that what we were experiencing was normal.

Long before going home, in the mix of all of the processes, learning experiences, metamorphoses and emotional changes we underwent, we had to learn how to handle simply "being there." The time we spent in country was a slice out of our lives. For some, it *was* life. Those serving in Vietnam had a widely accepted way of calculating the period of time they'd have to "be there" before going home. They counted backwards.

Among the greetings and salutations and "getting to know each other" processes that folks went through when they met was their "in-country" status as it related to time. An individual would introduce himself by name and how long it would be before he'd return to civilization. In addition to delineating how much longer a person had to serve, this status also signified how experienced they were, ostensibly how many close calls they'd survived, and more importantly, how much longer their luck had to hold out.

Things were a little different for those who signed up to do multiple tours, but for them, going home or even simple survival (in the sense that many had a sort of twisted death wish) wasn't a priority.

The newest folks in country referred to their identity and status as "365 and a wake-up" meaning they had to do 365 days and would head home on the day of the last time they would wake up in country. The clock began there and "ticked" backwards, and few were the individuals who didn't have a clear, concise count in their minds at all times.

The most common subject of idle conversation among us was what we'd do when we got back home, when all this was over and we could once again take up the process of simply growing old. It must be understood that while the normal evolution from childhood to young adulthood and the full, independent status of "grownup" with a profession and a wife and kids was expected by young people all across America, for those who went to Vietnam, that evolution was abandoned, and a new, relatively unknown developmental process replaced it.

Those destined to fight in the war took a giant leap over most of this "normal growing up" and landed in a place and time and developmental situation few could have described for them beforehand. As such, the roles they were to play were fairly obscure.

Young people back home were starting college or getting a job at the local gas station or beginning a career with Dad. Maybe they were getting their first apartments, falling deeper in love with their childhood sweethearts, and planning the next stage of their lives. They knew how to do these things. Dad had taught them what to expect and what was expected of them and how to respond to every detail of normal life. Even kids who joined the military but never went to war had an idea what would happen, what was expected of them, and how to fulfill these expectations.

For the rest of us, we were plucked out of "normalcy" at 17 or 18 and dropped unceremoniously into the chaos and turmoil that was Southeast Asia—Vietnam—without the benefit of a set of simple "manufacturer's instructions." We were in unexplored waters; all we had was each other. Everything we learned about life, the life we now led, came from the guys who had "225 and a wake-up" or had broken the "100 level" and were counting steadily down. The most knowledgeable, of course, were those guys who had less than a month or two left in country, but they rarely involved themselves with "new folks" for several reasons.

Complicating all this was timing. Most of the things that would eventually go bad in the Vietnam War were just beginning to take root and materialize in every negative way in the mid to late 60s. As for our relationship with the people of Vietnam, that honeymoon was just about over, and everyone was a little tired of the toothpaste cap being left off.

Back home, the young warriors returning from Vietnam were fast becoming "baby-killers," and the first wave of returning vets was routinely being spat upon at airports. Things were souring all across the board. For Jack and Billy and David and me, however, even then we had a plan to beat it all. Somehow, we had unfailing faith that things were going to be different for us.

Jack, David, and Billy had come into country together and were therefore slated to leave on the same flight out. I was to be a month behind them. When they broke "29 and a wakeup," our post-patrol, post-mission conversations around the Jack Daniels bottle began centering on leaving and getting back home. We weren't exactly packing our bags, but the excitement of leaving, and of course the apprehension related to all the things that could go wrong, took center stage. Above all, we were determined to stay together for the remainder of our lives. Even then, a small voice within us told us that we would need each other, though we didn't yet understand why.

A highly predictable thing happens when humans share near death experiences. People who were total strangers before the event are suddenly bound together. Deep, long-lasting friendships and annual reunions, just to talk, are common among people who have survived a catastrophic plane crash, for instance. Some scientists even insist that among these individuals exists the ability to communicate complex thoughts or feelings with only a shared glance. Such bonds are strong and long-lasting.

30. So, What Do We Do Now?

End-of-life experiences were virtually a daily occurrence for all who lived through combat in Vietnam. The bond that was formed among us was and is indescribable. For this reason, planning to maintain close connections and ties throughout life was as sacred as taking that last step off the soil of Vietnam onto the aircraft that would ferry us home.

I had maintained a correspondence with Jack's sister for some time and had already planned to marry her if she would accept me. For me, it was a natural, solid plan in which I would not only gain a beautiful wife, but become a member of a perfect family and have the father I'd grown up without.

The most important thing for all of us, however, was that the support we'd given each other and received from each other would continue. In actuality, though we refused to acknowledge it, we were afraid. The fear we felt was a fear of never being normal, a fear of never being able to regain the time we'd lost or our place among normal human beings. We were going to be "different," almost like a colony of lepers, and we knew it. We just didn't know how it was all going to play out, and it scared us a little bit.

Additionally, although we didn't know it at the time, once we got home, we would for years to come be searching for the things we'd left behind in Vietnam. For some, the search became permanent. That fruitless search would signal the ruination of many. Some would wind up in and out of jail. Some would see danger everywhere they went and be constantly ready to respond defensively. Some would channel this frustration into dangerous occupations, and ultimately, some would just keep going back until they came to a literal end of their quest.

For us, however, planning the actual logistics of our individual departures from country began to seep into whiskey-fueled discussions around the beginning of the last month before the three of them departed. The intellectual thought and planning that went into such minor things such as whether spare issue jungle boots should be polished before they were packed, or how and where we'd exchange Vietnamese piasters for U.S. dollars or whether we should keep some of it for old times' sake, were all sources of prime conversation that would last hours. We were like kids, albeit often inebriated kids, planning for Christmas morning.

"At least I won't have to be lugging that damn M14 around like you guys, haha!" Jack jibed David and Billy. "Godfrey took care of that for us."

Some weeks before, our boat had been upended in a firefight and was found drifting in the Mekong, bow out of the water. I had been "volunteered" to dive under it and come up inside to try to recover any weapons or sensitive items. Since the M14s belonging to me and Jack had hung from a weapons rack in the bow of the boat for the duration of our time in country and were hanging there still, I took the opportunity to give them an honorable burial at sea while underneath the bow, reporting them missing when I surfaced. Now, all we had to carry out of country was a "note" from "Dad," indicating they'd been lost in combat. I wasn't prone to waste, but took some solace in the fact that "lost in combat" was actually an honest summation, to a point.

"Yeah," I added jovially, "I'll come back when this is all over and go find them and clean them up as good as new."

"Hell," said David, "can you imagine how rich you'd be years from now if you could dredge that damn river. The brass alone would be worth billions."

"Shit, man," Billy said, "those damn guns have been carried halfway to San Francisco by the current by now."

"Wish *Godfrey* had thought about me and David," Billy chimed in, drawing my name out in a good-naturedly sarcastic, third person tone as if I weren't there. "Now we're gonna be humping that damn sea bag, all our separation papers and orders, and that damn 'M14' cannon."

David took a swig from the bottle, lit a cigarette, squinted, and pointed an instructional finger toward the three of us, holding our attention while he waited for the burn to subside so he could talk. "You know I musta fired a couple of million rounds since I've been here, and never once … never once," he emphasized, "have I fired a round through that M14 I was required to bring with me."

"Ha," Billy offered, "mine's got a family of mice living in the chamber."

"I didn't say I hadn't cleaned it," David offered. "I just hadn't fired it."

"Some of the Marines around here swear by theirs, you know," I said.

"Yeah," Jack said. "Just a waste for us though."

These daily contemplations of events that we expected would lead to departure from country were not always tinged with pleasant anticipation. A normal, emotional anchor chain hung around our necks. Though we hadn't known it at the time, it would hang there the rest of our lives, like the burden carried by Jacob Marley in *A Christmas Carol*. In those days, and all the coming days of our lives, happy thoughts of survival would be overshadowed by memories of friends who were lost and the guilt of the survivor, for some morphing from guilt to shame.

"Wish Musetti had made it out with us," Jack mused one evening a few days before their departure.

"Yeah, and Graham," David added. "Hell, I wish … never mind."

"They're resting here though," I said.

"Hell, they ain't here," Billy added with an unusual flash of annoyance. "I watched them both being flown out of here. They're both sleeping in the ground back home somewhere, and you know it."

"You're wrong," I replied. "None of us, alive or dead, will ever leave here."

"What the fuck are you talking about?" David asked, drawing out the "fuck" for appropriate emphasis.

"I'm just saying," I replied, "and you know it ain't a bad thing, but little pieces of all of us are scattered all around this country. Even if we do go home, it won't be 'whole.' A drop of blood here or a pound of flesh there, all have become as real a part of this country as if we'd fathered children here who'd remain here behind us, and even though I'm convinced that the immortal souls of Graham and Musetti and all the rest are safe with Jesus, I can't help but believe there's a little bit of the spiritual being of all of us, including Graham and Musetti and Lake and all of us, that will roam these damn jungles forever."

Following a contemplative pause, David laughed and chimed in, "Well at least I know damn well I didn't father no children here."

I waited for the predictable giggles and responses of, "Hell, nah" and "Fuckin' A, Bubba" died down.

"I'm just sayin' and hell, it ain't a bad thing, but the damn fact is, when you live somewhere, and you invest something in that place, and hell, you can't deny the investment we've all made here, the place just becomes part of you, and I'll say it again," I paused for emphasis. "You leave something there, something that grows and becomes as much a part of the place as if you'd been born and died there. Just sayin' … is all."

Finally, the "wake-up" morning came. Jack, Billy, and David threw their gear into the bed of the old Navy gray, dust-covered pickup truck at around 5 a.m. The truck was to take them to the pier where they would board a PBR that would ferry them to Vinh Long. There they would catch a chopper to Tan Son Nhut Airfield in Saigon, where they'd catch anything they could get on that was heading to Clark Air Base in the Philippines, and from there, on to California. Their trip, and mine a month later, would be in exact reverse order of the trip we had taken more than a year ago. Their "365 and a wake-up" had dwindled to the "wake-up" and now, that too had been accomplished.

Brothers in the Mekong Delta

As the driver of the pickup revved the engine impatiently, I embraced the three of them. As one would expect, the moment was filled with a multitude of emotions and was another first for all of us. Never before had we experienced such things or shared such experiences with others. Never before had we bonded so fervently with another human being outside our immediate family, and never before had we parted with those same human beings.

I couldn't help thinking that there should have been some sort of ceremonial process to mark the occasion. Instead, we just hugged and made some stammering comments about coming back together again soon and sharing all those coming events with each other, brothers forever. I don't know whether we all believed it or whether it was just a natural thing to say at a time like that. I do know we had spent untold hours those last few weeks planning the better part of our future lives and sketching out each moment, assuring that it would be a moment shared among us.

We swore never to lose touch or let a day pass without at least talking to each other. I didn't know it at the time, but brothers-in-arms had, throughout the history of wars, made those same promises to each other and had, at the time, meant every word. Only rarely, however, had the tug of the world and family not been successful in overriding such pledges.

Jack, David, and Billy touched down in California and were processed out within days. In addition to sharing their training and deployment experiences, they also coincidently shared an ETS (separation from the military) date. The military, for good and bad reasons, out-processes combat veterans returning to the States very quickly.

Their intentions are good in that they want to reunite veterans and their families as soon as possible. Their intentions are also somewhat self-serving in that they want to get rid of any potential issues relating to combat as quickly as possible. A returning veteran who is suffering from a combat-related issue or an addiction to drugs or alcohol may want to get help, but if they know they are going to have to stay behind to receive that help while their friends and fellow combat veterans are all going home, they're less likely to do so. In fairness, the military wants to help these veterans, but they aren't likely to prioritize the effort. A short out-processing timeline helps to put things off as long as possible, and young men carry their baggage home, anxious to become normal once again.

All too quickly, the three of them were saying goodbye, and for the first time in more than a year, were boarding separate means of transportation: Jack on a flight to Oklahoma City, Billy to Birmingham, and David to Charlotte,

North Carolina. The phone numbers they'd exchanged were put away for safekeeping and, like most things related to the war, in the excitement of getting home, were soon lost.

"For damn near 30 years," David said once at a reunion in subsequent years, "every time I saw a car or truck from Oklahoma, I looked closely hoping to see Jack at the wheel. I'd do the same thing when I'd see someone with Alabama plates, searching for Billy."

"Yeah," Jack replied. "I'd always get drunk and call every David Taylor in Charlotte and every Billy Moore in Birmingham. Use to drive Catina crazy."

Catina, Jack's only child, was born a few years after Vietnam and grew up devoted to him. Children and loved ones of Vietnam veterans almost always admire them and want to stay beside them, but doing so is difficult. Without realizing it, we all brought a disease back with us. Some of us were slightly afflicted while others were stricken and became debilitated.

Outward manifestations of the sickness were often, sadly, easy to see. Alcoholism, drug addiction, hatred and suspicion, even for those who loved us most, were common. For those who were only slightly less affected, the aforementioned manifestations were less visible, lurking just under the consciousness but eager to burst forth and destroy everything that is good. For those family members like Catina, even later in life, devotion to us is an act of bravery and sacrifice.

Over the years, we often lashed out at people, most of whom didn't deserve it. We knew in our hearts that we were unworthy of love and often grew frustrated with those who loved us the most because of it. It's almost impossible for someone who has experienced relentless combat and the stress and emotional effects of it to forgive others for not understanding. Of course, it's completely impossible for others to fully understand.

And for too many, the anger and frustration are eased somewhat by alcohol or drugs, but in the end such crutches only exacerbate the issue. Divorce and separation from children were common in those early years among returning Vietnam vets. It was also clear to us that rather than "the returning, conquering hero" to be hailed, we were more likely to be shunned and often denigrated. Such knowledge did little to ease the anger.

Jack fought a lot. All of us had trouble managing anything approximating relationships and could never understand that our efforts were stymied by the simple fact that we found it difficult not to be complete assholes. We were all searching desperately for an answer and could never grasp the possibility that there was no such thing. We just moved from one possible solution to another, in each case sabotaging anything positive that may result from any of them. All we really wanted to do was to reach back and grab some of those "normal" times we had lost. We wanted the time spent hanging out at the drive-in with friends or going to high school or college dances, or courting a sweetheart and making the same stupid "growing up" mistakes our friends had made, but we had given all that up. To us, we had given it up for something noble, and in the end should be rewarded or at least respected for it. We were, after all, the "good guys." We left as the "good guys" and would return the "good guys," but something just went wrong.

Almost thirty years from the day Jack, Billy, and David looked at each other on the tarmac at Travis AFB, said goodbye, and parted, David received a recorded phone message. A soft, seemingly sad female voice asked haltingly, "Is this the David Taylor that was in Vietnam and knew Jack Anderson?"

David had continued a steady, fruitless search for Jack and Billy over the years, and upon hearing the message, was completely convinced from the tone that Jack had passed away. He copied the number and started to dial, but stopped. He wasn't ready to hear. The following day he dialed again but hung up before there was an answer. Twice more, he called and hung up, as if reality would have been thwarted as long as he just didn't actually hear it. Finally, on the third day, he closed his eyes, gritted his teeth and waited until that same soft young girl's voice answered.

Hearing the "Hello," David burst out with, "I'm so sorry about Jack."

Sensing what was happening, Catina immediately shifted into a tone of excitement, "No, David, no; Daddy is fine. He's anxious to talk to you. He's right here."

So began a new era in the lives of us all. David and Jack pooled and redoubled their individual efforts to locate Billy. Once back in contact, they met often, soon widening their circle to include Bill Fuller, who'd become a preacher and musician who successfully recorded spiritual songs about Vietnam and the young men who fought there. Phil Yocum had also become a preacher, true to his word to God following the firefight that had taken the lives of Proffer, Prendergast, and Lake, and had very nearly taken his. Doyle Hensley, probably the youngest boat captain in Vietnam, and Don Rogers, the only one of us who still seemed to maintain the sense of optimism he'd always had in country, were soon rolled into the fold.

I had reentered the military, this time in the United States Army, Special Forces, staying long enough to retire and doing two tours in Afghanistan

in the process. They always kept me in the loop and made sure I knew that I was just as much a part of this select group as the day Jack had dragged me down to the bami-bar for a beer on my first day with the section back in country. Though I couldn't be with them every time they reunited over the years, I talked to them all regularly.

Soon after returning from country, I had married Jack's sister. I was finally part of that special family with the father I'd always wanted and a wife worthy of a king. Jack had married a similarly perfect mate, a marriage which produced his daughter, Catina. Two of the most perfect children anyone ever had were the result of my marriage to Jack's sister. Unfortunately neither Jack nor I was capable of being the husband and father we should have been and had eventually found ourselves alone once again.

Jack's reunion with Billy and David, however, led to his marrying Billy's wife's sister, a marriage which lasted till his death. Those years following the reunion of the three of them were a blessing to us all and have provided us with the healing, understanding, and support we'd searched for. A family that few can understand or explain was finally complete and remains so to

From left: **Jack Anderson and Billy Moore. They died within months of each other and rest today, reunited in the Mansions of the Lord.**

Left to right: David Taylor, Jack Anderson, Billy Moore and author. Maybe it was simple fate or a kind of love few people can understand, but Billy died in Birmingham in the spring of 2018, mere weeks after Jack passed away in the VA hospital there. As Jack lay on his deathbed at the hospital, Billy said to him, "Rest easy, brother. I'll see you soon." Billy's gentle assurance to Jack is one all Vietnam veterans understand perfectly: Rest easy, brothers. We'll all be together soon.

this day, even though Jack and Billy, having passed within a month of each other, are no longer here in body.

Jack and Billy both died peacefully in the spring of 2018. With the help and encouragement of Jack's daughter Catina, and the unending desire to be joined once again to relive, for a few short years, the joys and the sorrows of a period of time that defined us, we now recognize our worth and are proud of what we were as individuals and as brothers. God bless all who serve and have served and will serve this great country. We will meet again in the Mansions of our Lord.

Index

Index